Progressive Dispensationalism and the Missing Throne

Gerald B. Shugart

Lulu Publishing | Morrisville, North Carolina

PROGRESSIVE DISPENSATIONALISM

AND THE

MISSING THRONE

by:

Gerald B. Shugart

Formatting conducted by ShelfBloom ePress.
Concerns about formatting, typographical errors,
etc. should be sent to support@shelfbloom.com.

This book is dedicated to James Frank Beck, Jr., who was a friend when I really needed a friend.

"And now abideth faith, hope, charity, these three; but the greatest of these is charity."

Table of Contents

Chapter I

The Throne of David

1. Introduction

Traditional Dispensationalist Charles Ryrie wrote the following concerning the fact that the Progressive Dispensationalists teach that the Lord Jesus is now sitting upon the throne of David:

"One of the major departures, if not 'the' major one, of progressive dispensationalism from traditional dispensationalism and premillennial teaching is that Christ, already inaugurated as the Davidic king at His ascension, is now reigning in heaven on the throne of David." [1]

An examination of the facts concerning the Lord Jesus' ascension into heaven will prove that the Lord Jesus did not sit upon the throne of David at that time. When He ascended into heaven He was set down at the right hand of the heavenly throne of God:

"Now of the things which we have spoken

1

this is the sum: We have such an high priest,
who is set on the right hand of the throne
of the Majesty in the heavens" (Heb. 8:1).

"*Looking unto Jesus the author and*
finisher of our faith; who for the joy that
was set before him endured the cross,
despising the shame, ***and is set down at the***
right hand of the throne of God" (Heb.
12:2).

Darrell Bock, a Progressive
Dispensationalist, says that the throne of
David is set next to the Father:

"*The image of sitting on the throne is*
clearly an image of rule, and the description
of being seated next to the Father accords
with the language of Psalms 110, a
messianic Psalm. The previous texts in
Revelation make it clear that this is an
already bestowed authority. Furthermore,
this throne of the lamb, set next to the
father, *is alluded to again in Revelation*
22:1...Jesus is neither passive nor inactive
from ***his right hand throne***" [*emphasis*
added]. [2]

According to Bock the heavenly throne of
the Lord Jesus is the same throne as the
Davidic throne:

"*The Davidic throne and the heavenly throne of Jesus at the side of the Father are one and the same*, *but there are two stages to the rule from that throne*" [*emphasis added*].[3]

The Progressive Dispensationalists teach that the Lord Jesus is now in heaven sitting upon the throne of David and He has been sitting there since He ascended into heaven. But we will see that they are in error.

2. The Missing Throne

The Apostle John witnessed a scene set in the heavenly sphere and in the following passage he speaks of a throne which he saw there:

"*After this I looked, and, behold, a door was opened in heaven...And immediately I was in the spirit: and, behold, **a throne was set in heaven, and one sat on the throne**" (Rev. 4:1-2).

The one who sits upon the throne is Almighty God (v. 8) and John saw that that He had a book in his right hand:

"*And I saw in the right hand of him that sat on the throne a book written within and*

3

on the backside, sealed with seven seals"
(Rev. 5:1).

Then John saw the Lord Jesus take the book out of the right hand of God:

*"And I beheld, and, lo, in the midst of the throne and of the four beasts, and in the midst of the elders, **stood a Lamb** as it had been slain, having seven horns and seven eyes, which are the seven Spirits of God sent forth into all the earth. **And he came and took the book out of the right hand of him that sat upon the throne**"* (Rev. 5:6-7).

First notice that John saw the Lord Jesus "standing" and therefore at that time He was not sitting on any throne. Besides that, when John saw the Lord Jesus and God together he only saw one throne and it is God who is sitting upon that throne and not the Lord Jesus. And John speaks of both of them in the following verse and he speaks of only God being upon a throne:

"Blessing, and honour, and glory, and power, be unto him that sitteth upon the throne, and unto the Lamb for ever and ever" (Rev. 5:13).

If the Davidic throne is in heaven now

then why didn't John see it? John had a clear, unobstructed view of the heavenly scene, being able to see the throne of God and also able to see seven lamps of fire burning before God's throne (4:5). But he did not see any throne on the right hand of God's throne. He also saw four beasts at God's throne (Rev.4:6) and he counted twenty four elders around that throne (Rev.4:10) but he did not see a throne at the right hand of that throne.

Bock understands that the word "throne" signifies reigning or ruling. "*It should first be pointed out,*" he says, "*that 'throne' is a pictorial description for rule...*" [4]

Since John saw no throne that can only mean that the Lord Jesus is not now reigning and the Messianic kingdom is not now in existence. The following words of the Lord Jesus make that fact certain because He said that the kingdom will not even be near until He returns to the earth:

"***And then shall they see the Son of man coming in a cloud with power and great glory***. *And when these things begin to come to pass, then look up, and lift up your heads; for your redemption draweth nigh. And he* *spake to them a parable; Behold the fig tree, and all the trees; When they now shoot forth, ye see and know of your own selves that summer is now nigh at hand. So likewise ye,* **when ye see these things come to pass, know ye that the kingdom of God is nigh at hand**" (Lk. 21:27-31).

The Progressive Dispensationalists assert that the Messianic kingdom is now in existence despite the fact that the Lord Jesus said in no uncertain terms that it wouldn't even be near until He returns to the earth. They also teach that the Lord Jesus sat upon the throne of David when He ascended into heaven but the Lord Jesus says that He will not sit upon that throne until He returns to the earth:

"**When the Son of man shall come in his glory**, *and all the holy angels with him,* **then shall he sit upon the throne of his glory**" (Mt. 25:31).

The meaning of the Greek word translated "then" in this instance is "*of things future ; 'then'...when the things under discussion takes place*" [5]

At Matthew 25:31 the Lord tells us exactly "when" He will sit upon His throne and that is "when" He shall come in His glory. The Progressive Dispensationalists teach that He is already sitting upon His throne but if that is true then why would the Lord say that He will sit upon His throne when He returns to the earth?

These facts prove beyond any doubt whatsoever that the Lord Jesus is not now upon the throne of David and that He will not begin to reign from the throne of David until He returns to the earth. These facts are irrefutable and undeniable. This is not the only evidence from the Scriptures which prove that the Messianic kingdom is not now in existence so we will now look at more evidence.

3. The Kingdom Age

In the following two passages the Lord Jesus spoke of two different ages, the "age" in which He was then living and an "age to come":

*"'Truly I tell you,' Jesus said to them, 'no one who has left home or wife or brothers or sisters or parents or children for the sake of the kingdom of God will fail to receive many times as much in **this age, and in the age to come eternal life**'"* (Lk. 18:29-30;

7

NIV).

"*'Truly I tell you,' Jesus replied, 'no one who has left home or brothers or sisters or mother or father or children or fields for me and the gospelwill fail to receive a hundred times as much in* **this present age***: homes, brothers, sisters, mothers, children and fields--along with persecutions--***and in the age to come eternal life*" (Mk. 10:29-30; NIV).

The "age to come" is the kingdom age and in the following verse John the Baptist spoke of it as being near:

"*In those days came John the Baptist, preaching in the wilderness of Judaea, And saying, Repent ye:* **for the kingdom of heaven is at hand**" (Mt. 3:1-2).

In *The Oxford Dictionary of the Jewish Religion* we read that the term "kingdom of heaven" is "*an eschatological concept referring to a future state of perfection in the world, free from sin and suffering, in which all will live in accordance with the divine will. 'Heaven' is a metonymy for 'God'; the term thus refers not to a heavenly realm but to the kingdom of God on earth.*" [6]

In the following verse the Lord Jesus told His disciples to pray for it to come to the earth:

"*When ye pray, say, Our Father which art in heaven, Hallowed be thy name. **Thy kingdom come**. Thy will be done, as in heaven, so in earth*" (Lk. 11:2).

The age to come is the kingdom age. In the book *Four Views On the Book Of Revelation* Progressive Dispensationalist Marvin Pate speaks of the "age to come" being the kingdom age and then says that age appeared at the coming of the Lord Jesus:

"*The best understanding of the Gospels-- the Olivet Discourse included--is that Jesus' utterances about the Kingdom of God were partially fulfilled at his first coming (the already aspect). When all is said and done, this is the most viable solution to both the quest for the historical Jesus and the apparent delay of the Second Coming. In other words, just as Jesus promised, **the age to come did indeed dawn in his coming**, but within the context of this present age...according to Revelation **the kingdom of God (the age to come) has dawned in***

9

*heaven" [emphasis added]. *[7]

In the following passage the Lord Jesus speaks of the things which will happen at the "end of the age" in which He was then living and the same age which precedes the kingdom age, the "age to come":

*"Then Jesus sent the multitude away and went into the house. And His disciples came to Him, saying, 'Explain to us the parable of the tares of the field.' He answered and said to them: 'He who sows the good seed is the Son of Man. The field is the world, the good seeds are the sons of the kingdom, but the tares are the sons of the wicked one. The enemy who sowed them is the devil, **the harvest is the end of the age**, and the reapers are the angels. Therefore as the tares are gathered and burned in the fire, so it will be at **the end of this age.** The Son of Man will send out His angels, and they will gather out of His kingdom all things that offend, and those who practice lawlessness, and will cast them into the furnace of fire"* (Mt. 13:36-42; NKJV).

All of the unbelievers will be taken out of the world at the end of the age, the age which will precede the kingdom age. And that will leave only those who are born again to populate the Messianic kingdom:

"*Jesus answered and said unto him, Verily, verily, I say unto thee, Except a man be born again, he cannot see the kingdom of God...Except a man be born of water and of the Spirit, he cannot enter into the kingdom of God*" (Jn. 3:3,5).

From these facts we can know that the Kingdom age has not yet appeared because before that happens there will be a world wide harvest when all of the unbelievers on the earth will be weeded out. The Progressive Dispensationalists teach that the kingdom age is already here despite the fact that the end of the age which will precede that age still remains in the future. Again, we see facts from the Scriptures which forbid the idea that the Messianic Kingdom is now in existence. Next, we will examine what the Apostle Paul said about the kingdom.

4. His Appearance And His Kingdom

Paul taught that the Lord Jesus' kingdom remained in the future when he wrote the following:

"I charge thee therefore before God, and the Lord Jesus Christ, who shall judge the quick and the dead at his appearing and his kingdom" (2 Tim. 4:1).

Here we see that Paul places the kingdom age in the future at the appearing of the Lord Jesus when He will judge the living and the dead. In the following verse Paul speaks of the judgment of the living at the Lord Jesus' appearance:

"And then the lawless one will be revealed, and the Lord Jesus will slay him with the breath of his mouth and destroy him by his appearing and his coming" (2 Thess. 2:8; RSV).

"And to you who are troubled rest with us, when the Lord Jesus shall be revealed from heaven with his mighty angels, In flaming fire taking vengeance on them that know not God, and that obey not the gospel of our Lord Jesus Christ" (2 Thess. 1:7-8).

Besides that, while the Lord walked the earth He spoke of a future judgment of those in the grave (Jn.5:28-29) in regard to their resurrection and here He speaks of the time when the believers will be raised from the dead:

12

"And this is the will of him that sent me, that every one which seeth the Son, and believeth on him, may have everlasting life: and I will raise him up at the last day" (Jn. 6:40).

The believers will be raised from the dead at the last day, the last day which will precede the age to come, the kingdom age. According to Paul the kingdom age remains in the future and that matches the Lord Jesus' words at Luke 21:27-31 when He said that His kingdom won't even be near until He returns to the earth.

The words of both Paul and the Lord Jesus about the time when the kingdom will be set up on the earth directly contradict the teaching of Progressive Dispensationalism that the Lord Jesus is now reigning from the Davidic throne.

5. Thy Throne Shall Be Established Forever

From the very beginning the throne of David was established as an earthly throne because Solomon sat upon that throne on the earth:

"Then sat Solomon upon the throne of

13

David his father; and his kingdom was established greatly" (1 Ki. 2:12).

According to the promise which God made to David that earthly throne was established for ever:

"*And thine house and thy kingdom shall be established for ever before thee: **thy throne shall be established for ever**"* (2 Sam. 7:16).

Since David's earthly throne has been established for ever then there will never be a time when the throne of David will be anything other than an earthly throne. God also said that He would not "alter" the promises which He made to David:

"*I have made a covenant with my chosen, **I have sworn unto David my servant**... Nevertheless my loving-kindness will I not utterly take from him, nor suffer my faithfulness to fail. My covenant will I not break, **nor alter the thing that is gone out of my lips**. Once have I sworn by my holiness that I will not lie unto David*" (Ps. 89:3,33-35).

The Progressive Dispensationalists teach that the LORD did indeed alter the things which He promised David because according to them the earthly throne did not remain an earthly throne but instead it became a heavenly throne and then it will revert back to being an earthly throne.

There is no such thing as a throne of David located in heaven and that explains why John did not see that throne when he was given a vision of the throne room of God. The scheme developed by the Progressive Dispensationalists is entirely dependent on the idea that the Lord Jesus is now in heaven sitting upon the throne of David. According to them the kingdom is already here because the Lord Jesus is now sitting on the throne of David in heaven. They say that the kingdom is here already despite the fact that the Lord Jesus said that it would not even be near until he returns to the earth.

6. The Tabernacle of David

Let us look at the following prophecy which the Lord Jesus will fulfill when He returns to the earth:

*"In that day will **I raise up again the tabernacle of David that is fallen down; and I will build again the ruins thereof,***

and I will set it up...That the residue of men might seek after the Lord, and all the Gentiles, upon whom my name is called, saith the Lord, who does all these things" (Amos 9:11-12; Septuagint).

As soon as David became king of Israel he sought to bring the Ark of the Covenant back to the people so he raised up a tabernacle or tent where he could place the Ark:

*"And David made him houses in the city of David, **and prepared a place for the ark of God, and pitched for it a tent**"* (1 Chron. 15:1).

The "throne of David" was located in the "tabernacle of David":

*"And in mercy **shall the throne be established: and He shall sit upon it in truth in the tabernacle of David**, judging, and seeking judgment, and hasting righteousness"* (Isa. 16:5).

Now let us look at the following prophecy again:

"In that day will I raise up again the tabernacle of David that is fallen down; and

16

I will build again the ruins thereof, and I will set it up" (Amos 9:11-12; *Septuagint*).

This prophecy will be fulfilled when the Lord Jesus restores the house or family of David by ruling from the throne of David. It will happen "in that day." Later, at the Jerusalem council at Acts 15, James quotes Amos 9:11-12 and makes a change to that prophecy (in 'bold') and by that change we can know that the Lord Jesus will not raise up again the tabernacle of David and sit upon the throne of David until He returns to the earth:

"***After this I will return***, *and will build again the tabernacle of David, which is fallen down; and I will build again the ruins thereof, and I will set it up: That the residue of men might seek after the Lord, and all the Gentiles, upon whom my name is called, saith the Lord, who doeth all these things*" (Acts 15:16).

The Lord Jesus will not sit upon the throne of David until the tabernacle of David is raised up again and that will not happen until He returns to the earth. This is more evidence that the Progressive Dispensationalists are in error when they teach that the Lord Jesus is now sitting upon the throne of David.

Summary

The Progressive Dispensationalists overlook the fact that before the Lord Jesus will usher in the Messianic kingdom the great tribulation must happen first. The following passages demonstrate that fact:

"Behold, the eyes of the Lord GOD are upon the sinful kingdom, and I will destroy it from off the face of the earth; saving that I will not utterly destroy the house of Jacob, saith the LORD...In that day will I raise up the tabernacle of David that is fallen, and close up the breaches thereof; and I will raise up his ruins, and I will build it as in the days of old" (Amos 9:8,11).

"For then shall be great tribulation, such as was not since the beginning of the world to this time, no, nor ever shall be...When the Son of man shall come in his glory, and all the holy angels with him, then shall he sit upon the throne of his glory" (Mt. 24:21,25:31).

"Then shall the LORD go forth, and fight against those nations, as when he fought in

the day of battle. And his feet shall stand in that day upon the mount of Olives...And the LORD shall be king over all the earth: in that day shall there be one LORD, and his name one" (Zech. 14:3-4,9).

Besides that, if the Messianic kingdom exists now then it would make absolutely no sense for the Lord Jesus to say that it will not even be near until He returns to the earth. If the Lord Jesus began to sit upon His throne when He ascended into heaven then it would make no sense for Him to say that He will not sit upon that throne until He returns to the earth. When given a vision of the throne room of God the Apostle John saw the Lord Jesus standing and he did not see any throne which belongs to Him, much less the throne of David. That fact alone denies the teaching of the Progressive Dispensationalists. The throne of David was established for ever as an earthly throne so it defies reason to assert that it is in heaven now. Despite all of this Scriptual evidence the Progressive Dispensationalists teach that the kingdom age is already here so we must believe that the kingdom age is an evil age.

"Grace and peace to you from God our Father and the Lord Jesus Christ, who gave

19

*himself for our sins to rescue us from **the present evil age**, according to the will of our God and Father"* (Gal. 1:3-4; NIV).

All of these facts provide overwhelming evidence that the Lord Jesus is not now sitting upon the throne of David and therefore the kingdom age has not yet arrived.

There's a ZERO chance that the Lord Jesus is now sitting upon the throne of David and therefore there is a ZERO chance that the teaching of Progressive Dispensationalism is correct.

Later I will answer the Scriptures which the Progressive Dispensationalists think prove that the Lord Jesus is now sitting on the throne of David. But next I want to address the circumstances which lead to the entrance of Progressive Dispensationalism into the Dispensational Community.

End Notes

1. Charles C. Ryrie, *Dispensationalism* (Chicago, IL: Moody Press, 1995), 167.

2. Darrell L. Bock, "The Reign of the Lord Christ" in *Dispensationalism, Israel*

and the Church ed. Craig A. Blaising and
Darrell L. Bock (Grand Rapids: Zondervan
Publishing House, 1992), 63.

3. *Ibid.*, 63-4.

4. *Ibid.*, 51.

5. Joseph Henry Thayer, *A Greek-English
Lexicon of the New Testament*" (Grand
Rapids: Baker Book House, 1977), 629.

6. *The Oxford Dictionary of the Jewish
Religion* ed. Adele Berlin (New York:
Oxford University Press, 2011), 428.

7. C. Marvin Pate, "A Progressive
Dispensationalist View of Revelation," in
Four Views On The Book Of Revelation, ed.
C. Marvin Pate (Grand Rapids: Zondervan
Publishing House, 1998), 175.

Chapter II

The New Covenant

1. Progressive Dispensationalism Enters the Scene

One of the foundational teachings upon which Traditional Dispensationalism has been built is that the Body of Christ is an intercalation or parenthesis in the divine purposes toward Israel. The founding President of Dallas Theological Seminary, Lewis Sperry Chafer, correctly understood that the Body of Christ is "*wholly unrelated to any divine purpose which precedes it or follows it*":

"*But for **the Church intercalation -- which was wholly unforeseen and is wholly unrelated to any divine purpose which precedes it or which follows it**. In fact, the new, hitherto unrevealed purpose of God in the outcalling of a heavenly people from Jews and Gentiles is so divergent with respect to the divine purpose toward Israel, which purpose preceded it and will yet follow it, that the term parenthetical, commonly employed to describe the new age-purpose, is inaccurate. **A parenthetical portion sustains some direct or indirect relation to that which goes before or that which follows; but the present age-purpose is not thus related and therefore is more properly termed an intercalation**" [emphasis added].[1]

In the 1980's a group of dispensationalists who had started to question the teaching of the Traditional Dispensationalists such as Chafer and Charles Ryrie denied the Church parenthesis and asserted that those in the Body of Christ partake of the New Covenant (Jeremiah 31:31) promised to the nation of Israel.

Ryrie says that progressive dispensationalism *"has modified or clouded the classic, normative, dispensational dictinction between Israel and the church...by abandoning the concept of the church as an intercalation or parenthesis. Classic dispensationalism used the words 'parenthesis' or 'intercalation' to describe the distinctiveness of the church in relation to God's program for Israel. An intercalation is an insertion of a period of time in a calendar, and a parenthesis in one sense is defined as an interlude or interval (which in turn is defined as an intervening or interruptive period). So either or both words can be appropriately used to define the church age if one sees a distinct interlude in God's program for Israel (as clearly taught in Daniel's prophecy of the seventy weeks in 9:24-27)"* [emphasis added]. [2]

The dispensationalists who questioned the teaching of Chafer and Ryrie came to the conclusion that those in the Body of Christ partake of the spiritual blessings of Israel's New Covenant and thus they rejected the idea of the Church parenthesis.

Walter C. Kaiser, Jr., wrote that "*when Israel and the church were viewed as sharing one and the same covenant the possibilities for major rapprochement between covenant theology and dispensationalism became immediately obvious.*" [3]

This "major rapprochement" came into existence in the form of Progressive Dispensationalism, as witnessed by the title of the book authored by Robert Saucy:

The Case for Progressive Dispensationalism: **The Interface Between Dispensational and Non-Dispensational Theology**.

Ryrie wrote the following about the progressive dispensationalism movement: "*Two professors at Dallas Theological Seminary, Darrel L. Bock (New Testament) and Craig A. Blaising (Systematic Theology), have been in the forefront of this movement, along with Robert L. Saucy (Systematic Theology) of Talbot Theological Seminary...in the overall historical picture of dispensational theology, this new movement inaugurates an era clearly distinguished from previous eras of dispensational thought.*" [4]

Next, we will examine the New Covenant promised to the nation of Israel to see if those in the Body of Christ partake of that covenant in any way whatsoever.

2. The New Covenant in the Old Testament

The following passage is the only place in the OT where we find the words "new covenant":

*"Behold, the days come, saith the LORD, that I will make a **new covenant** with the house of Israel, and with the house of Judah: **Not according to the covenant that I made with their fathers in the day that I took them by the hand to bring them out of the land of Egypt; which my covenant they brake**, although I was an husband unto them, saith the LORD: But this shall be the covenant that I will make with the house of Israel; After those days, saith the LORD, I will put my law in their inward parts, and write it in their hearts; and will be their God, and they shall be my people. And they shall teach no more every man his neighbour, and every man his brother, saying, Know the LORD: **for they shall all know me, from the least of them unto the greatest of them, saith the LORD: for I will forgive their iniquity, and I will remember their sin no more**" (Jer. 31:31-34).*

The LORD says that He will make a New Covenant with the house of Israel and the house of Judah. The "fathers" of those who will partake of this covenant were the children of Israel whom the Lord redeemed out of Egypt and the same people who broke His covenant (Jer.11:1-8). Since the "fathers" of these future members of the houses of Israel and Judah were the physical descendants of Abraham, Isaac and Jacob then that can only mean that in the future the members of both houses will also be the physical descendants of Abraham, Isaac

25

and Jacob. So in the future there will be a generation made up of the physical descendants of Jacob (Israel) who will all know the LORD and all of them will have their sins forgiven and be saved. Since that has never happened in the past that explains why Paul put the fulfillment of this prophecy in the future:

"And so all Israel shall be saved: as it is written, There shall come out of Sion the Deliverer, and shall turn away ungodliness from Jacob: For this is my covenant unto them, when I shall take away their sins" (Ro. 11:26-27).

From this we know that the fulfillment of the New Covenant remains in the future because there has never been a time when all of the physical descendants of Israel knew the LORD and had their sins forgiven--*"for they shall all know me, from the least of them unto the greatest of them, saith the LORD: for I will forgive their iniquity, and I will remember their sin no more."*

The Two Programs of God Are Mutually Exclusive

When the nation of Israel was in covenant relationship with God circumcision was a requirement for the sons of Israel and any uncirumcised male was cut off from that nation:

"This is my covenant, which ye shall keep, between me and you and thy seed after thee; Every man child among you shall be circumcised. And ye

shall circumcise the flesh of your foreskin; and it shall be a token of the covenant betwixt me and you...And the uncircumcised man child whose flesh of his foreskin is not circumcised, that soul shall be cut off from his people; he hath broken my covenant" (Gen. 17:10-11,14).

On the other hand, circumcision profits no one during the Church age, as witnessed by Paul's words here:

"*For in Jesus Christ neither circumcision availeth any thing, nor uncircumcision; but faith which worketh by love*" (Gal. 5:6).

The Scriptures reveal that when the nation of Israel was in a covenant relationship with the LORD the children of Israel were a special people unto Himself:

"*For thou art an holy people unto the LORD thy God: **the LORD thy God hath chosen thee to be a special people unto himself, above all people that are upon the face of the earth***" (Deut. 7:6).

On the other hand, during the Church age there are no special people unto the LORD except for believers and in the Body of Christ there is no distinction between the Jews and those of other nationalities:

"*And have put on the new man, which is renewed in knowledge after the image of him that created him: **Where there is neither Greek nor Jew,***

27

circumcision nor uncircumcision, *Barbarian,
Scythian, bond nor free: but Christ is all, and in all"*
(Col. 3:10-11).

Norman L. Geisler writes the following about
Colossians 3:10-11:

*"In Christ distinctions are removed. These
include national distinctions (**Greek or Jew**...);
religious distinctions (**circumcised or
uncircumcised**)..."* [5]

These facts serve to prove that when the LORD's
program for Israel is in view then that program
cannot be about the Body of Christ because His two
different programs are mutually exclusive. In other
words, when the Divine plan toward Israel is in
effect then the children of Israel are above all
people on the face of the earth so therefore it is
impossible that at the same time the Divine plan is
also toward the Body of Christ where there is no
difference between the Jews and the Gentiles. Sir
Robert Anderson wrote the following:

*"For just as we aver that 'God cannot lie,' we
may assert that He cannot act at the same time
upon two wholly different and incompatible
principles."* [6]

When the LORD is dealing with the Body of
Christ His program toward Israel is in abeyance.
Also, a sharp divide is seen at the end of the church
age when the saints will be caught up to meet the
Lord Jesus in the air. Once that happens the Body of

28

Christ will be removed from the earth and that will pave the way for Israel to be restored to her previous position as a people above all people on the face of the earth.

These facts support the idea of a Church parenthesis because the Divine purpose toward Israel is wholly unrelated to the Divine purpose toward the Body of Christ. Therefore we can understand that the New Covenant promised to Israel has nothing to do with the Body of Christ because the two Divine programs are mutually exclusive.

The New Covenant which was promised to Israel has not yet been fulfilled because there has never been a time when all of the physical descendants of Israel have known the LORD and had their sins forgiven. No one today or in the past has received any of the spiritual blessings which will flow from that covenant in the future.

3. The New Covenant and Gentile Salvation

In his book *The Case For Progressive Dispensationalism* Robert Saucy says that "***the Old Testament prophecies, the promise of salvation under the new covenant, and the promises to Abraham and David all contained provisions for the blessing of the nations along with Israel.*** *This blessing of the nations was ascribed to the messianic era.* ***This era has arrived***, *according to the New Testament, and thus the promises of the*

29

New Covenant have begun to take effect and are available to all who will receive the Messiah" [*emphasis added*]. [7]

Saucy is correct that the OT prophecies of the New Covenant contain provisions for the blessing of the Gentiles. However, he is in error when he says that the era of these prophesised blessings for the Gentiles has arrived. In the same book on page 112 Saucy says that the words "everlasting covenant" found in the following two passages are speaking of the "new covenant":

*"For I the LORD love judgment, I hate robbery for burnt offering; and I will direct their work in truth, and I will make **an everlasting covenant** with them. And their seed shall be known among the Gentiles, and their offspring among the people: all that see them shall acknowledge them, **that they are the seed which the LORD hath blessed**"* (Isa. 61:8-9).

*"Incline your ear, and come unto me: hear, and your soul shall live; and I will make **an everlasting covenant** with you, even the sure mercies of David...Behold, thou shalt call a nation that thou knowest not, and nations that knew not thee shall run unto thee because of the LORD thy God, and for the Holy One of Israel; **for he hath glorified thee**"* (Isa. 55:3,5).

These OT prophecies reveal that the Gentiles will receive blessings through the agency of Israel at a time when the nation will be restored to Divine favor and at a time when the LORD will glorify and bless that nation. That certainly is not happening now and it has not happened at anytime in the past. The following prophecy speaks of the time when the New Covenant will be in force and the nation of Israel will be a blessing to the world and it will be the Jews who will bring the world unto the knowledge of Christ:

*"And I will bring them (Israel), and they shall dwell in the midst of Jerusalem: and they shall be my people, and I will be their God, in truth and in righteousness...And it shall come to pass, **that as ye were a curse among the heathen, O house of Judah, and house of Israel; so will I save you, and ye shall be a blessing**...In those days it shall come to pass, that ten men shall take hold out of all languages of the nations, **even shall take hold of the skirt of him that is a Jew, saying, We will go with you: for we have heard that God is with you**"* (Zech. 8:8,13,23).

These prophecies regarding Gentile salvation are not now being fulfilled so no one in the Body of Christ has received any spiritual blessings as a result of the New Covenant. The Apostle Paul says that salvation has come to those in the Church as a result of the fall of Israel:

*"I say then, Have they stumbled that they should fall? God forbid: but rather **through their fall salvation is come unto the Gentiles**, for to provoke*

31

them to jealousy. Now if the fall of them be the riches of the world, and the diminishing of them the riches of the Gentiles; how much more their fulness?" (Ro. 11:11-12).

The spiritual blessings enjoyed by those in the Body of Christ are not received through the agency of Israel so therefore those blessings have nothing to do with the New Covenant. Saucy is in error when he writes that *"according to the Scriptures, the salvation of God that flows from the Cross is given to all mankind through the new covenant."* [8]

At the Cross the Lord Jesus ratified the New Covenant with His blood but *"He came unto his own, **and his own received him not**"* (Jn. 1:11).

Since the nation of Israel did not believe that the Lord Jesus is her promised Messiah the New Covenant remains unfulfilled. Despite this fact Progressive Dispensationalist Bruce Ware speaks of a "preliminary nature of the new covenant's fulfillment":

"The preliminary nature of the new covenant's fulfillment can be seen in two ways. First, only the spiritual aspects of new-covenant promise are now inaugurated in this age; the territoral and political aspects, though part of God's new-covenant promise, await future fulfillment." [9]

The Scriptures will be searched in vain for any evidence which speak of both a "preliminary" and a "future" nature of the New Covenant's fulfillment.

Besides that, the only party who will receive any spiritual blessings which will flow through the New Covenant will be the children of Israel.

Don Trest writes that "***Recognition of the 'Israel only' aspect of the New Covenant is the single most important exegetical key to understanding the New Covenant***. *This permits a consistemt application of literal grammatical-historical (let-it-say-what-it-says) methodology to the reading of the text of the New Covenant (thus eliminating any need to view the New Covenant as being fulfilled by the Church in the present Church age - spiritual or otherwise). To put the Church into the New Covenant muddies the interpretive waters and diminshes exegetical clarity (because it is based in artifical already not yet allegorical-theological hermeneutical schemes). Moreover, any unauthorized (forced) mixture of Israel and the Church (based on a non-literal or allegorical-theological reading of the New Covenant) changes the meaning and message of the Bible and disfigures the revelation given to Man in the Bible. This does disservice to the Word of God, discounts the faithfulness of God, and dishonors His name*" [emphasis added].* [10]

The New Covenant is not being fulfilled now so no one is receiving any benefits from that covenant. Despite this fact Robert Saucy asserts that Paul is now a minister of the New Covenant to those in the Body of Christ:

"The presence of the reality of the Old Testament promise of the new covenant is also seen in Paul's identification of himself as a minster of 'a new covenant' to the church at Corinth (2Co. 3:6)" [11]

Here is the translation of the verse which Saucy cites:

"He has made us competent as ministers of a new covenant--*not of the letter but of the Spirit; for the letter kills, but the Spirit gives life*" (2 Cor. 3:6; NIV).

According to the Saucy's understanding of this verse Paul is a minister of the New Covenant and that covenant is bringing spiritual life to others. However, as pointed out earlier, no one at this time is receiving any blessings from the New Covenant because it remains unfulfilled. Also, as pointed out earlier, when the LORD is in covenant relationship with Israel then the children of Israel are a people above all people on the face of the earth. But in the Body there is no distinction between the Jews and other people. So we can understand that when the Divine plan is in regard to Israel then it is impossible that at the same time the Divine plan is in regard to the Body of Christ. The two Divine plans of God are mutually exclusive.

Next we will look at the correct translation of 2 Corinthians 3:6.

4. Ministers of the New Testament

34

Here is the correct translation:

"*Who also hath made us able **ministers of the new testament (diathēkē)**; not of the letter, but of the spirit: for the letter killeth, **but the spirit giveth life**"* (2 Cor. 3:6; KJV).

John Calvin understood that Paul was speaking of the ministry to preach the gospel, writing the following:

"*'Not of the letter but of the spirit'...There is, however, no doubt, that by the term 'letter,' he means the Old Testament, as **by the term 'spirit' he means the gospel**; for, after having called himself a 'minister of the New Testament,' he immediately adds, by way of exposition, that he is a 'minister of the spirit,' and contrasts the letter with the spirit"* [*emphasis added*]. [12]

A.R. Fausset also understands that Paul is referring to the ministry of the gospel and not a ministry of the New Covenant:

"*spirit giveth life--**The spirit of the Gospel** when brought home to the heart by the Holy Spirit, **gives new spiritual life to a man** (Ro 6:4, 11)"* [*emphasis added*]. [13]

The following two verses speak of the "ministry" and the "Spirit" which gives life spoken of at 2 Corinthians 3:6:

"*But none of these things move me, neither count I my life dear unto myself, so that I might finish my*

35

course with joy, and **the ministry**, *which I have
received of the Lord Jesus,* **to testify the gospel of
the grace of God**" (Acts 20:24).

"*It was revealed to them that they were not
serving themselves but you, when they spoke of the
things that have now been told you by those* **who
have preached the gospel to you by the Holy Spirit
sent from heaven**" (1 Pet. 1:12; NIV).

Therefore, we can understand that when Paul
uses the word *diathēkē* at 2 Corinthians 3:6 the
meaning of that word is the New Testament, the
gospel. Now let us look at the meaning of the Greek
word translated "testament" at 2 Corinthians 3:6.

According to Joseph Henry Thayer the Greek
word *diathēkē* means "*a disposition, arrangement,
of any sort, which one wishes to be valid...***esp. 'the
last disposal' which one makes of his earthly
possessions after his death, a 'testament' or 'will'**"
[*emphasis added*]. [14]

So one of the meanings of the Greek word
diathēkē is "testament" or "will," as in the Last Will
and Testament of Christ. J. H. Moulton and G.
Milligan say that Greek word "*is properly
'dispositio,' an 'arrangement' made by one party
with plenary power, which the other party may
accept or reject, but cannot alter.* **A 'will' is simply
the most conspicuous example of such an
instrument**, *which ultimately monopolized the word
just because it suited its differentia so completely*"

[*emphasis added*]. [15]

From these facts we can understand that the ministry of the New *Diathēkē* is the ministry of the Last Will and Testament of Christ which is the same thing as the ministry of the gospel of Christ. Therefore, we can understand that when Paul used the word *diathēkē* at 2 Corinthians 3:6 his reference was to the "gospel of Christ".

William Beck wrote the following about Martin Luther's idea that the Greek word *diathēkē* carries the meaning of the "gospel":

*"For Luther the 'berith' of the Old Testament was, in essence, the Gospel-promise of Jesus Christ, while **the 'diathēkē' was the Gospel-promise completed in the Christ** who was already born, sacrificed, risen, and who was coming again to give His people the ultimate inheritance: forgiveness of sins in heaven. This is why he writes: **'And so that little word 'testament' is a short summary of all God's wonders and grace, fulfilled in Christ'** (LW:XXXV:84)"* [*emphasis added*]. [16]

Those in the Body of Christ receive their spiritual blessings through the Last Will and Testament of Christ, the gospel of Christ. Next, we will see that the verses which follow 2 Corinthians 3:6 also demonstrate the same truth, that in Paul's mind the *diathēkē* of which he is given the ministry is the gospel.

5. The New *Diathēkē* is the Gospel of Christ

37

Once again, in the following verse Paul speaks about Christians being ministers of the "New Testament" or New *Diathēkē*:

"*Who also hath made us able **ministers of the new testament (diathēkē)**; not of the letter, but of the spirit: for the letter killeth, but the spirit giveth life*" (2 Cor. 3:6; KJV).

In the next chapter Paul speaks about that same ministry and from his words we can understand that the ministry is in regard to preaching the gospel of Christ:

"***Therefore seeing we have this ministry**, as we have received mercy, we faint not; But have renounced the hidden things of dishonesty, not walking in craftiness, nor handling the word of God deceitfully; **but by manifestation of the truth** commending ourselves to every man's conscience in the sight of God. But if **our gospel** be hid, it is hid to them that are lost: In whom the god of this world hath blinded the minds of them which believe not, lest the light of **the glorious gospel of Christ**, who is the image of God, should shine unto them. **For we preach not ourselves, but Christ Jesus the Lord**"* (2 Cor. 4:1-4).

Paul's words "this ministry" are obviously pointing back to the "ministry" of 2 Cor.3:6 and his words "this ministry" are in regard to the "*manifestation of the truth,*", the preaching of "*Christ Jesus the Lord*"-- "***the glorious gospel of Christ.***"

So we can understand that when Paul speaks of the ministry of the New Testament he is speaking of the ministry of the gospel. Albert Barnes wrote the following commentary on 2 Corinthians 4:1:

*"**Seeing we have this ministry - The gospel ministry**, so much more glorious than that of Moses...which is the ministry by which the Holy Spirit acts on the hearts of people...which is the ministry of that system by which people are justified...and which is the ministry of a system so pure and unclouded"* [*emphasis added*]. [17]

A.R. Fausset wrote the following about 2 Corinthians: *"seeing we have this ministry 'The ministration of the Spirit' (2 Co 3:8, 9): **the ministry of such a spiritual, liberty-giving Gospel**: resuming 2 Co 3:6, 8"* [*emphasis added*]. [18]

Since we know that the words "this ministry" are referring to the preaching of the gospel and those same words are referring to the ministry of "the New Testament" mentioned at 3:6 then we know that both are referring to a ministry of the gospel. Therefore, we can understand that in Paul's mind when he used the word *diathēkē* when applying it to the Body of Christ his reference was to the gospel which comes in the Holy Spirit:

*"**For our gospel** came not unto you in word only, but also in power, and **in the Holy Spirit**, and in much assurance; as ye know what manner of men we were among you for your sake"* (1 Thess. 1:5).

So once again we see that the spiritual blessings

which those in the Body of Christ receive are a result of the Last Will and Testament of Christ, the gospel of Christ, and not through the New Covenant promised to Israel.

T. M. Morris wrote: "*Having considered Christ as the testator,* **let US NOW LOOK AT THE GOSPEL AS THE 'LAST WILL AND TESTAMENT OF CHRIST'**...*There is, in every testament, provision implied or expressed that it should, with all convenient speed, be published and made known. This is necessary, that the legatees may become aware of that which has been bequeathed to them, and be in a position to put in their claim.* **Christ has ordained and provided that His disciples should publish His will and testament to all the children of men. We are 'put in trust with the gospel.' We are bound to publish the glad tidings in every direction**" [*emphasis added*]. [19]

6. "Testament" in the Book of Hebrews

The following passage demonstrates that the blessings which those in the Body of Christ receive is as a result of the Last Will and Testament of Christ:

"*For this reason Christ is the mediator of **a new diathēkē**, that those who are called may receive the promised eternal inheritance--now that he has died as a ransom to set them free from the sins committed under the first covenant. In the case of a will, it is necessary to prove the death of the one*

40

*who made it, because a will is in force only when
somebody has died; it never takes effect while the
one who made it is living*" (Heb. 9:15-17; NIV).

As already demonstrated, when the word
"diathēkē is used in regard to those in the Body of
Christ the meaning of that word is "testament" so
here is the correct translation of this passage:

"*For this reason Christ is the mediator of **a new
testament**, that those who are called may receive
the promised eternal inheritance--now that he has
died as a ransom to set them free from the sins
committed under the first covenant. **In the case of a
will, it is necessary to prove the death of the one
who made it, because a will is in force only when
somebody has died; it never takes effect while the
one who made it is living**"* (Heb. 9:15-17).

Henry Alford wrote that "*It is quite vain to deny
the testamentary sense of 'diathēkē' in this verse....I
believe it will be found that we must at all hazards
**accept the meaning of 'testament,' as being the
only one which will in any way meet the plain
requirement of the verse**"* [*emphasis added*]. [20]

Elliott E. Johnson writes that "*when the writer
then begins to talk about the inauguration of the
'diathēkē' (vv. 16,17), **he describes it is functioning
as a last will and testament**. This is indicated
because the arrangement begins to function at the
death of the 'testator' (v. 16). His explanation
means that a will and testament is in force when the
author of the will dies. **The inauguration of a will**

41

and covenant occurs on different bases. A covenant is inaugurated during the lifetime of both partners. Only a last will is inaugurated at the death of the author of the will" [*emphasis added*]. [21]

The Promised Eternal Inheritance

At Hebrews 9:15 the promise which is in regard to the New *Diathēkē* is about an "inheritance," and under a Last Will and Testament it is the "heirs" who receive this inheritance. That is in accordance with the Scriptures which declares that one becomes a heir by the Lord Jesus' Last Will and Testament, the gospel:

"*That the Gentiles should be **fellowheirs**, and of the same body, **and partakers of his promise in Christ by the gospel**"* (Eph. 3:6).

Kenneth S. Wuest wrote that "*the word 'inheritance' in 9:15 leads the inspired pensman to define the content of 'diathēkē' as it is used in this epistle. An inheritance involves the idea of someone making an disposition of his property, the heir receiving the same at the death of the testator...**in verse 15 the writer speaks of the Messiah as the Mediator of the New Testament who made that Testament effective through His death, and in that way, lost sinners who accept salvation on the terms of the will or testament come into their inheritance**"* [*emphasis added*]. [22]

Sir Robert Anderson taught that the Christian's

42

spiritual blessings are not received through a covenant but instead through a testament:

"Our spiritual and eternal blessings do not depend on a covenant made with us, but upon a testament under which we are beneficiaries." [23]

Let's look at this verse again:

*"For this reason Christ is the mediator of a new testament, **that those who are called may receive the promised eternal inheritance**--now that he has died as a ransom to set them free from the sins committed under the first covenant"* (Heb. 9:15).

The eternal inheritance is received upon being "called" and no one is called by the New Covenant promised to Israel but instead by the gospel:

*"Whereunto **he called you by our gospel**, to the obtaining of the glory of our Lord Jesus Christ"* (2 Thess. 2:14).

In his commentary on Hebrews 9:15-22 Matthew Henry wrote that *"In these verses the apostle considers the gospel under the notion of a will or testament, the new or last will and testament of Christ...."* [24]

Once again we see that the *diathēkē* which is operational today and applies to those in the Body of Christ is the Last Will and Testament of Christ, the gospel of Christ. Today no one receives spiritual blessings through the New Covenant promised to Israel but instead through the gospel of Christ

"For I am not ashamed of the gospel of Christ: for it is the power of God unto salvation to every one that believeth" (Ro. 1:16).

7. The Lord's Supper

Let us first look at the two different translations of the following words of the Lord Jesus spoken on the eve of the Cross in the Upper Room where He connects His "blood" or death to a *diathēkē*:

*"Then he took a cup, and when he had given thanks, he gave it to them, and they all drank from it. **'This is my blood of the covenant (diathēkē),** which is poured out for many,' he said to them"* (Mk. 14:23-24; NIV).

*"And he took the cup, and when he had given thanks, he gave it to them: and they all drank of it. And he said unto them, **This is my blood of the new testament (diathēkē),** which is shed for many"* (Mk. 14:23-24; KJV).

When the Lord Jesus said those words the Greek word *diathēkē* carried with it two different meanings. One of the meanings was in regard to the New Covenant which the LORD promised to the nation of Israel and the other meaning was in regard to the Lord Jesus' Last Will and Testament--the gospel.

The Meaning of *Diathēkē* on the Eve of the Cross

In the Upper room the disciples would have

44

understood that the Lord Jesus was speaking about the New Covenant promised to the nation of Israel. Robert B. Chisholm, Jr., recognizes the fact that on the day of Pentecost the coming of the Millennium remained in view:

"*When he (Peter) observed the outpouring of the Spirit **on the day of Pentecost he rightly viewed it as the first stage in the fulfillment of Joel's prophecy**. Apparently he believed that the kingdom was then being offered to Israel and that **the outpouring of the Holy Spirit signaled the coming of the Millennium**. However, the complete fulfillment of the prophecy (with respect to both the extent of the Spirit's work and the other details) **was delayed because of the Jewish unbelief**" [emphasis added]. [25]*

Robert L. Saucy recognizes the fact that the New Covenant will be fulfilled in the Millennium, writing that "*the connection between the new covenant and the kingdom is evident in Jesus' teaching that his work, which throughout Scripture is intimately identified with **the coming of the kingdom, is also the fulfillment of the new covenant**. In fact, **Jesus expressly tied the fulfillment of the Passover, which he celebrated with his disciples, to the coming of the kingdom of God** (Lk 22:16, 18; cf. Mt 26:29; Mk 14:25)*" [emphasis added]. [26]

Saucy correctly notes that the Lord Jesus' words in the upper room tied the fulfillment of Israel's New *Diathēkē* to the earthly kingdom.

The Meaning of *Diathēkē* in the Lord's Supper

It was only later after Paul was converted that an understanding of the meaning of the significance of the Lord's Supper for the present dispensation was given. Paul received a special revelation (*"I have received of the Lord..."*) about the meaning of the Lord's Supper which is not related to the kingdom:

*"**For I have received of the Lord that which also I delivered unto you,** That the Lord Jesus the same night in which he was betrayed took bread: And when he had given thanks, he brake it, and said, Take, eat: this is my body, which is broken for you: this do in remembrance of me. After the same manner also he took the cup, when he had supped, saying, This cup is the new testament in my blood: this do ye, as oft as ye drink it, in remembrance of me. **For as often as ye eat this bread, and drink this cup, ye do shew the Lord's death till he come**"* (1 Cor. 11:23-26).

The coming of the Lord Jesus spoken of here is not in regard to His returning to the earth to set up the earthly kingdom. Instead, the following verse speaks of an "imminent" appearance of the Lord Jesus:

*"You too, be patient and stand firm, because **the Lord's coming is near**"* (James 5:8; NIV).

The Greek word translated "is near" at James 5:8 is *eggizo* and in this verse that word means *"to be imminent."* [27]

The Lord Jesus' appearance is described as being "imminent" so that appearance can happen at any moment. Therefore it has nothing whatsoever to do with the Lord Jesus' return to the earth to set up the earthly kingdom because before that can happen the abomination of desolation must first stand in the holy place (Mt.24:15). That "coming" of the Lord Jesus cannot be described as being "imminent." For more on this subject please go to Appendix #2.

From these facts we know that when Paul quoted the Lord Jesus' words which He spoke on the eve of the Cross the meaning which he placed on the word *diathēkē* was "testament" and not "covenant":

*"After the same manner also he took the cup, when he had supped, saying, **this cup is the new testament (diathēkē) in my blood**: this do ye, as oft as ye drink it, in remembrance of me. For as often as ye eat this bread, and drink this cup, **ye do shew the Lord's death till he come**"* (1 Cor. 11:25-26; KJV).

John Frahm III wrote that *"**the use of the word 'testament' confesses more fully the Gospel promises and cross-focused content of Christ's person and work** that is distributed Sunday after Sunday in the Divine Service"* [emphasis added]. [28]

8. The Mediator of the New Testament

The Greek word translated "mediator" is *mesites*, and one of the meanings of that word is "*a medium of communication, arbitrator...used of Moses, as one who brought the commands of God to the people of Israel and acted as a mediator with God on behalf of the people."* [29]

The Lord Jesus is the Prophet who served as the medium of communication between the Father and the people:

*"I will raise them up a Prophet from among their brethren, like unto thee, **and will put my words in his mouth; and he shall speak unto them all that I shall command him**"* (Deut. 18:18).

It was in His role of Prophet when He began to reveal truths which are essential to the gospel:

*"Very truly I tell you, whoever hears my word and **believes** him who sent me **has eternal life** and will not be judged but has crossed over from death to life"* (Jn. 5:24).

The Lord's words there are in regard to the eternal inheritance spoken of here:

*"Therefore, He is the mediator of a new testament, **so that those who are called might receive the promise of the eternal inheritance**"* (Heb. 9:15).

The Lord also revealed this truth concerning His death:

*"Even as the Son of man came not to be ministered unto, but to minister, and **to give his life a ransom for many**"* (Mt. 20:28).

During his ministry Paul received communications from the Lord Jesus in regard to His Last Will and Testament, the gospel. Here we read the following about how he received the gospel from the Lord Jesus:

*"But I certify you, brethren, that **the gospel** which was preached of me is not after man. For I neither received it of man, neither was I taught it, **but by the revelation of Jesus Christ** "* (Gal. 1:11-12).

We also read Paul's words here which speak of further revelations which He received from the Lord Jesus:

*"It is not expedient for me doubtless to glory. **I will come to visions and revelations of the Lord**...And lest I should be exalted above measure through **the abundance of the revelations**, there was given to me a thorn in the flesh, the messenger of Satan to buffet me, lest I should be exalted above measure"* (2 Cor. 12:1,7).

Therefore, it is in the sense of being a medium of communication that the Lord Jesus is described as being a Mediator of the New Testament.

John Chrysostom sums up the Lord Jesus' role as a Mediator, saying *"How did He become Mediator? He brought words from Him and brought them to us, conveying over what came from the Father to us, and adding His own death thereto."* [30]

9. The Book of Hebrews

The first thing to remember is that every time when the author of Hebrews refers to a *diathēkē* which is operational today the reference is to the Last Will and Testament of Christ, the gospel of Christ.

Hebrews 7:22

"By so much was Jesus made a surety of a better testament (diathēkē)" (Heb. 7:22).

The Lord Jesus is now the surety of a better *diathēkē,* and that *diathēkē* is the Last Will and Testament of Christ, the gospel of Christ. A surety can be described as a guarantee and the Lord Jesus is the guarantee of the truth and terms of the Last Will and Testament of Christ, the gospel of Christ. That is because He is faithful in fulfilling His promises (Heb. 10:23).

Hebrews 8:6

"But now hath he obtained a more excellent ministry, by how much also he is the mediator of a better testament (diathēkē), which was established upon better promises" (Heb. 8:6).

As already shown the Lord Jesus is the Mediator of a better *diathēkē* and that *diathēkē* is the Last Will and Testament of Christ.

Hebrews 8:7-10

"For if that first covenant had been faultless, then should no place have been sought for the second. For finding fault with them, he saith,

Behold, the days come, saith the Lord, when I will
make a new covenant with the house of Israel and
with the house of Judah: Not according to the
covenant that I made with their fathers in the day
when I took them by the hand to lead them out of
the land of Egypt; because they continued not in my
covenant, and I regarded them not, saith the Lord.
For this is the covenant that I will make with the
house of Israel after those days, saith the Lord; I
will put my laws into their mind, and write them in
their hearts: and I will be to them a God, and they
shall be to me a people" (Heb. 8:7-10).

There is no evidence that when the author quotes
Jeremiah 31:31-34 that he is saying that the second
diathēkē is now in force.

John Walvoord understands this to be true,
writing that "*The argument hangs on the point that*
the Mosaic covenant was not faultless-was never
intended to be an everlasting covenant (Heb. 8:7).
In confirmation of this point, the new covenant of
Jeremiah is cited at length, proving that the Old
Testament itself anticipated the end of the Mosaic
law in that a new covenant is predicted to supplant
it...A further statement is made that the old
covenant is 'becoming old' and is 'nigh unto
vanishing away.' **It should be noted that nowhere**
in this passage is the new covenant with Israel
declared to be in force. The only argument is that
which was always true-the prediction of a new
covenant automatically declares the Mosaic
covenant as a temporary, not an eternal covenant"

[*emphasis added*]. [31]

Hebrews 9:15-16

"*For this reason Christ is the mediator of a new diathēkē, that those who are called may receive the promised eternal inheritance--now that he has died as a ransom to set them free from the sins committed under the first diathēkē. In the case of a diathēkē, it is necessary to prove the death of the one who made it*" (Heb. 9:15-16).

It has already been shown that Christ is the Mediator of the Last Will and Testament of Christ, the gospel of Christ. And in this passage we read that He is the Mediator of this Last Will and Testament so that "*those who are called may receive the promised eternal inheritance.*"

Those who are called receive the promised eternal "inheritance," and an inheritance is an integral part of any last will and testament. Besides that, no one is called by the New Covenant promised to Israel but instead the calling is by the gospel:

"*Whereunto he called you by our gospel, to the obtaining of the glory of our Lord Jesus Christ*" (2 Thess. 2:14).

Hebrews 10:9-10

"*Then said he, Lo, I come to do thy will, O God. He taketh away the first diathēkē, that he may establish the second diathēkē. By the which will we are sanctified through the offering of the body of Jesus Christ once for all"* (Heb.10:9-10).

The first *diathēkē*, the law, was taken out of the way as far as a person's righteous standing before the LORD and now all those who believe the gospel receive the imputed righteousness which is of God:

"For Christ is the end of the law for righteousness to every one that believeth" (Ro. 10:4).

"But to him that worketh not, but believeth on him that justifieth the ungodly, his faith is counted for righteousness" (Ro. 4:5).

Hebrews 10:16-19

"This is the covenant that I will make with them after those days, saith the Lord, I will put my laws into their hearts, and in their minds will I write them; And their sins and iniquities will I remember no more. Now where remission of these is, there is no more offering for sin. Having therefore, brethren, boldness to enter into the holiest by the blood of Jesus" (Heb. 10:16-19).

There is nothing here that even hints that the New Covenant promised to the nation of Israel is in force today. The sins of believers today are forgiven when saved by believing the New *Diathēkē* which is in force today--the Last Will and Testament of Christ, which is the gospel of Christ.

Hebrews 12:24

"And to Jesus the mediator of the new testament, and to the blood of sprinkling, that speaketh better things than that of Abel" (Heb. 12:24).

Again, it has been demonstrated that the Lord Jesus is the Mediator of the Last Will and Testament of Christ, the gospel of Christ.

10. Spiritual Blessings Under Israel's New Covenant

Craig A. Blaising wrote that *"It is indisputable that the New Testament views the new covenant predicted by Jeremiah and Ezekiel as established in the death of Jesus Christ with some of the promised blessings now being granted to Jews and Gentiles who are believers in Jesus.* ***These are not blessings which are 'like' those predicted by Jeremiah and Ezekiel. They are 'the very same' blessings which those prophets predicted.*** *For the new covenant which is presently in effect through Jesus Christ is not one which is 'like' that predicted by Jeremiah and Ezekiel, but is 'that very same' covenant which they prophesised which is in effect today"* [*emphasis added*]. [32]

First of all, it has already been shown that no one today or in the past have received any blessings from the New Covenant because that covenant remains unfulfilled. So we know that Blaising is in error when he asserts that the same blessings promised under the New Covenant are the very same blessings which "individual" believers receive. Even before the promise of Israel's New

54

Covenant was made known believers were receiving the imputed righteousness which is of God, as witnessed by the following verses:

"By faith Noah, being warned of God of things not seen as yet, moved with fear, prepared an ark to the saving of his house; by the which he condemned the world, **and became heir of the righteousness which is by faith**" (Heb. 11:7).

"Abraham believed God, **and it was counted unto him for righteousness**" (Ro. 4:3).

The forgiveness of sins for "individual" Israelites was not dependent in any sense on the fulfillment of Israel's New Covenant. We can see that "individual" Jews had their sins forgiven before the New Covenant was ratified at the Cross. The Lord Jesus said the following to a woman who anointed His feet with oil:

"And he said unto her, **Thy sins are forgiven.** *And they that sat at meat with him began to say within themselves, Who is this that forgiveth sins also? And he said to the woman,* **Thy faith hath saved thee**; *go in peace*" (Lk. 7:48-50).

The "individual" salvation of both Noah and Abraham was not dependent on the New Covenant in any sense whatsoever. And since all believers down through the ages have received the same imputed righteousness then their salvation is not dependent on the New Covenant.

Roy Beachman writes that "*if Israelites under the*

55

'old' covenant could place their faith in God and experience the same spiritual blessings as predicted under the 'new' covenant, what is 'new' about the new covenant? **These spiritual benefits do not come into 'existence' with the enactment of the new covenant. Rather, these spiritual benefits find 'universal application' with the enactment of the new covenant.** *These blessings will not be the experience of 'some' Israelites, as they were under the old covenant.* **These blessings will be the experience of 'all' Israelites under the new covenant...under the new covenant, the 'universality' of Israel's salvation is 'new,' not salvation itself"** [*emphasis added*]. [33]

Beachman is correct that the blessings which will flow from the New Covenant will find a "universal application." Arnold Fruchtenbaum understands that the future "national regeneration" of Israel is tied to the New Covenant and it is in regard to a "total national regeneration":

*"**The basis of Israel's final regeneration is the New Covenant in Jeremiah 31:31-34**...The result of the New Covenant will be **a total national regeneration of Israel**...That Israel was to undergo **a national regeneration** is not confined to the words of the New Covenant alone. The truths of the New Covenant are greatly elaborated by various prophets"* [*emphasis added*]. [34]

Homer A. Kent, Jr., writes that *"the **essence of the new covenant is spiritual regeneration**, enjoyed now **by Christian believers** and prophesied* *for national Israel* at the second coming of Christ."[35]

Kent realizes that the spiritual regeneration for Israel is "corporate" in nature. Therefore, common sense dictates that no one today is sharing this corporate spiritual blessing which is promised to Israel. So the Progressive Dispensationalists are in error when they assert that today's spiritual blessings are the same ones spoken of in the prophecies about Israel's New Covenant.

Bruce Ware understands that the "forgiveness of sins" under Israel's New Covenant is corporate in nature, writing that "*Israel still awaits a future action of God whereby **he will bring 'all Israel' (Rom. 11:26), or the nation of Israel as a whole, under the provision of forgiveness of sins** and Spirit-indwelling...*" [emphasis added]. [36]

J. Bruce Compton also sees the same truth which Ware expressed:

"*The **promised deliverance encompasses the nation as a whole**...the term 'Israel' refers to national, ethnic Israel, and the expression 'all Israel' refers to the nation as a whole...Paul's point is that just as a remnant is presently experiencing salvation, so one day 'all Israel' will be saved'...the **nation's sins being forgiven** in his citation of Isaiah 27:9 in 11:27b, 'When I take away their sins'*" [emphasis added]. [37]

With this in view we can understand that the "forgiveness of sins" under Israel's New *Diathēkē* is corporate in nature and therefore it is not the same spiritual blessing enjoyed by the "individual" believer today.

George Eldon Ladd supports this idea when he wrote that "*in the Old Testament the eschatological salvation is always pictured in terms of **the national, theocratic fate of the people of Israel**" [emphasis added]. [38]

These facts clearly contradict Bruce Ware's assertion here concerning the preliminary fulfillment of Israel's New Covenant:

"*The preliminary nature of the new covenant's fulfillment can be seen in two ways. First, **only the spiritual aspects of new-covenant promises are now inaugurated in this age;** the territorial and political aspects, though part of God's new-covenant promise, await future fulfillment. The fulfillment of God's new covenant thus should not now be viewed as an all-or-nothing affair. Rather, it is best seen as partially fulfilled now (spiritual aspects of forgiveness and the indwelling Spirit for all covenant participants) and later to be realized in its completeness (when all Israel is saved and restored to its land).*" [39]

In regard to the spiritual aspects under the new covenant Charles Ryrie wrote that "*even progressives have to admit that certain of those blessings can only be partially realized today. For instance, the promise of the new covenant 'to remove the heart of rebellion' and give us 'hearts fully compliant' is not fulfilled today in the experience of believers. The progressives' need to qualify the fulfillment as being 'not fully free' from resistance to God's will and is not at all similiar to the promise of the new covenant (to remove rebellion)."* [40]

Summary

The New *Diathēkē* which has an application to those in the Body is not the New Covenant promised to Israel but instead it is the Last Will and Testament of Christ, the gospel of Christ. In the second epistle to the church at Corinth the Apostle Paul revealed that the New *Diathēkē* which applies to those in the Church is the "gospel" (2 Cor.3:6, 4:1-6). Then nearly five hundred years ago Martin Luther taught that the *diathēkē* which applies to those in the Body of Christ is the gospel. Then later Matthew Henry saw the same truth. In the 19th century dispensationalist Sir Robert Anderson taught that the Christian's spiritual blessings are not received through a covenant but instead through a testament.

Since then this precious truth has slipped through the fingers of the Traditional Dispensationalists. And as a result the theology put forth by the Progressive Dispensationalists has found a home at Dallas Theological Seminary and other seminaries and is gaining new converts every day.

Darrell Bock writes that *"In the Old Testament the fulfillment of the new covenant is tied to the inauguration of the kingdom."* [41]

Since the New Covenant promised to Israel has not been fulfilled then the Messianic kingdom has not yet come into existence. Now I will address the verses which the Progressive Dispensationalists employ in their failed attempt to try to prove that the kingdom is already here.

End Notes

1. Lewis Sperry Chafer, *Systematic Theology* (Dallas: Dallas Seminary, 1948) 4:41; 5:348-349.

2. Charles C. Ryrie, *Dispensationalism*, 134.

3. Walter C. Kaiser, Jr., "An Epangelical Response," in *Dispensationalism, Israel and the Church*, 369.

4. Charles C. Ryrie, *Dispensationalism*, 161-2.

5. Norman L. Geisler, "Colossians," in *The Bible Knowledge Commentary; New Testament* ed. John F. Walvoord and Roy B. Zuck (Colorado Springs: ChariotVictor Publishing, 1983), 681.

6. Sir Robert Anderson, *Forgotten Truths* (Grand Rapids: Kregel Publications, 1980), 44.

7. Robert Saucy, *The Case For Progressive Dispensationalism* (Grand Rapids: Zondervan, 1993), 138.

8. *Ibid.*, 111.

9. Bruce A. Ware, "The New Covenant and the

People(s) of God," in *Dispensationalism, Israel and the Church*, 94-5.

10. Don Trest, "Concluding Thoughts: the New Covenant Matters," in *An Introduction to the New Covenant,* ed. Christoper Cone (Hurst, TX: Tyndale Seminary Press, 2013), 366.

11. Robert Saucy, *The Case For Progressive Dispensationalism*, 126.

12. John Calvin, *Commentaries*, Accessed April 20, 2018. http://biblehub.com/commentaries/calvin/2_corinthians/3.htm.

13. A.R. Fausset, *Jamieson-Fausset-Brown Bible Commentary*, Accessed May 11, 2018. https://www.blueletterbible.org/Comm/jfb/2Cr/2Cr_003.cfm?a=1081006.

14. Joseph Henry Thayer, *A Greek-English Lexicon of the New Testament*, 136.

15. J.H. Molton and G. Milligan, *The Vocabulary of the Greek Testament* (Grand Rapids: Eerdmans, 1930), 148.

16. William Beck, *The New Testament: God's Word to the Nations*, (Cleveland: Biblion Publishing, 1988), 533-34.

17. Albert Barnes, *Barnes' Notes on the Bible*, Accessed May 12, 2018. http://www.sacred-texts.com/bib/cmt/barnes/co2004.htm.

18. A.R. Fausset, *Jamieson-Fausset-Brown Bible*

Commentary, Accessed May 11, 2018.
https://www.blueletterbible.org/Comm/jfb/2Cr/2Cr_
004.cfm?a=1082001).

19. T. M. Morris, *Christ's Last Will and Testament*, Accessed May 15, 2018.
http://biblehub.com/sermons/auth/morris/christ
%27s_last_will_and_testament.htm

20. Henry Alford, *The Greek Testament* (London: Rivingtons, Waterloo Place, 1863) IV:173, 174; cf. the renderings of ASV, RSV.

21. Elliott E. Johnson, "The Church Has an Indirect Relationship to the New Covenant" in *Dispensational Understanding of the New Covenant* ed. Mike Stallard (Schaumburg, IL: Regular Baptist Books, 2012), 172.

22. Kenneth S. Wuest, *Hebrews in the Greek New Testament for the English Reader* (Grand Rapids: Eerdmans Pub. Co., 1956), 165.

23. Sir Robert Anderson, *Types in Hebrews* (Grand Rapids: Kregel, 1978), 56.

24. Matthew Henry, *Commentary on the Whole Bible*, Accessed May 15, 2018. http://biblehub.com/
commentaries/mhcw/hebrews/9.htm

25. Robert B. Chisholm, Jr., "Joel" in *The Bible Knowledge Commentary; Old Testament*, 1421.

26. Robert L. Saucy, *The Case For Progressive Dispensationalism*, 133.

27. *A Greek English Lexicon, Liddell & Scott* (Oxford: Clarendon Press, 1940), 467.

28. John Frahm III, *The Lord's Supper as Christ's Last Will and Testament*, Accessed April 27, 2018. http://steadfastlutherans.org/2013/03/the-lords-supper-as-christs-last-will-and-testament/.

29. John Henry Thayer, *A Greek-English Lexicon of the New Testament*, 401.

30. *Homilies on the Gospel of St. John and the Epistle to the Hebrews by St. Chrysostom; Homily XVI* ed. Phillip Schaff, (Grand Rapids: Christian Classics Ethereal Library), 736.

31. John Walvoord, "The New Covenant with Israel," *Bibliotheca Sacra*, 110 (July 1953), 201.

32. Craig A.Blaising & Darrell L. Bock, *Progressive Dispensationalism* (Grand Rapids: Baker Books, 1993), 202.

33. Roy E. Beachman, "The Church Has No Legal Relationship to or Participation in the New Covenant" in *Dispensational Understanding of the New Covenant* (Schaumburg, IL: Regular Baptist Books, 2012), 116.

34. Arnold G. Fruchtenbaum, "Israel in the Messianic Kingdom," Accessed May 15, 2018. http://www.ldolphin.org/otpremill.html.

35. Homer A. Kent, Jr., "The New Covenant and the Church," *Grace Theological Journal*, 6:2, Fall, 1985, 290.

36. Bruce Ware, "The New Covenant and the People(s) of God," in *Dispensationalism, Israel and the Church*, 96.

37. J. Bruce Compton, "Dispensationalism, the Church, and the New Covenant," *Detroit Baptist Seminary Journal* (Fall, 2003), 27.

38. George Eldon Ladd, *The Last Things* (Grand Rapids: Wm. B. Eerdmans Publishing Co., 1978), 8.

39. Bruce Ware, *Dispensationalism, Israel and the Church*, 94-95.

40. Charles C. Ryrie, *Dispensationalism*, 170-171.

41. Darrell L. Bock, *Dispensationalism, Israel and the Church*, 43.

Chapter III

Progressive Dispensationalism and the Messianic Kingdom

1. Was the Kingdom Inaugurated at the Lord Jesus' First Coming?

Darrell Bock says that "*The kingdom is inaugurated with Jesus' first coming...throughout the survey of the kingdom concept in Luke's gospel, passages keep appearing that set forth the kingdom as present.*" [1]

If the kingdom was established when the Lord Jesus walked the earth then why would He tell His disciples to pray in the following way?:

"*And he said unto them, When ye pray, say, Our Father which art in heaven, Hallowed be thy name. Thy kingdom come. Thy will be done, as in heaven, so in earth*" (Lk. 11:2).

If the Lord had already inaugurated the kingdom and it was already on the earth then the Lord's instructions to His disciples about how to pray would make no sense whatsoever. After all, why would He tell them to pray for the kingdom to come to the earth if it was already there in the Person of the Lord Jesus Christ?

Another thing which must be pointed out is that the Scriptures reveal that a king's reign or rule does not begin until he sits upon the throne of his kingdom. Bock certainly understands this principle when he wrote the following:

*"It should first be pointed out that **'throne' is a pictorial description for rule**..."* [2]

Despite this fact Bock has the Lord Jesus reigning in His kingdom before He sits upon His throne. He singles out both Luke 11:20 and Luke 17:21 as evidence that the kingdom's arrival is declared even while the Lord Jesus walked the earth:

*"Once, on being asked by the Pharisees when the kingdom of God would come, Jesus replied, 'The coming of the kingdom of God is not something that can be observed, nor will people say, 'Here it is,' or 'There it is,' because **the kingdom of God is in your midst**"* (Lk. 17:20-21).

Later, however, when the Lord Jesus appeared before Pilate shortly before the Cross, He made it plain that His kingdom is not now of the world:

*"Jesus answered, **My kingdom is not of this world**: if my kingdom were of this world, then would my servants fight, that I should not be delivered to the Jews: **but now is my kingdom not from hence**"* (Jn. 18:36).

The Progressive Dispensationalists say that the kingdom was on the earth when the Lord Jesus walked the earth even though shortly before the Cross He said that "now" His kingdom is not of this world. The Progressive Dispensationalists fail to realize that at Luke 11:20 figurative language was being used to enable the listeners to understand that the Lord Jesus is the promised King and not to unequivocally declare that the promised kingdom was actually on the earth. When the Lord Jesus spoke about the kingdom being in the midst he was employing a figure of speech known as **Metonymy** or **Change of Noun**: "*When one name or noun is used instead of another, to which it stands in a certain relation...when the subject is put for something pertaining to it.*" [3]

Those who heard the Lord Jesus say that the kingdom is in the midst would know from the Old Testament Scriptures that the kingdom was not on the earth so they would understand that the Lord was using figurative language. He used the noun "kingdom" in the place of "king" so that those hearing Him would come to the conclusion that He was claiming to be the promised King of Israel.

2. Acts 2:30-35 and Psalm 110

Robert Saucy wrote the following concerning both Psalm 110 and Acts 2:

"*The meaning of the 'right hand of God' in Psalm110:1 and Acts 2:33 is, therefore, the position of messianic authority. It is the throne of David.*" [4]

Bock also attempts to tie the throne of David to Psalm 110, writing that "*The image of sitting on the throne is clearly an image of rule, and the*

67

description of being seated next to the Father accords with the language of Psalm 110, a messianic psalm." [5]

At Acts 2:33 Peter does indeed tie what he said at Acts 2:33 to Psalm 110:

"Therefore being by the right hand of God exalted, and having received of the Father the promise of the Holy Ghost, he hath shed forth this, which ye now see and hear. For David is not ascended into the heavens: **but he saith himself, The LORD said unto my Lord, Sit thou on my right hand, Until I make thy foes thy footstool"** (Acts 2:33-35).

The root of the error of Progressive Dispensationalism stems back to their misunderstanding of what David said at Psalm 110:

"The LORD said unto my Lord, Sit thou at my right hand, until I make thine enemies thy footstool... **The Lord at thy right hand shall strike through kings in the day of his wrath. He shall judge among the heathen, he shall fill the places with the dead bodies; he shall wound the heads over many countries"** (Ps. 110:1,5-6).

Here David is saying that the Lord Jesus, the Lord at the right hand, will *"strike through kings in the day of his wrath"* and *"he shall wound the heads over many countries."* When we examine the prophecies which speak of this activity of the Lord Jesus we can know that these things will happen prior to the Lord Jesus reigning from David's

68

throne:

"For I will gather all nations against Jerusalem to battle; and the city shall be taken, and the houses rifled, and the women ravished; and half of the city shall go forth into captivity, and the residue of the people shall not be cut off from the city. **Then shall the LORD go forth, and fight against those nations, as when he fought in the day of battle.** *And his feet shall stand in that day upon the mount of Olives, which is before Jerusalem on the east...And it shall be in that day, that living waters shall go out from Jerusalem; half of them toward the former sea, and half of them toward the hinder sea: in summer and in winter shall it be.* **And the LORD shall be king over all the earth**" (Zech. 14:2-4,8-9).

Before the Lord Jesus will be the king over all the earth He will strike through the kings of the world and David made it clear that had not yet happened at the time when the Lord Jesus was sitting at the right hand of God:

"The LORD said unto my Lord, Sit thou at my right hand, until I make thine enemies thy footstool... **The Lord at thy right hand shall strike through kings in the day of his wrath.** *He shall judge among the heathen, he shall fill the places with the dead bodies; he shall wound the heads over many countries"* (Ps. 110:1,5-6).

Therefore, we know that Peter's words in the following passage are speaking about things which

69

will happen prior to the time when the Lord Jesus will sit upon the Davidic throne:

"***Therefore being by the right hand of God exalted***, *and having received of the Father the promise of the Holy Ghost, he hath shed forth this, which ye now see and hear. For David is not ascended into the heavens:* ***but he saith himself, The LORD said unto my Lord, Sit thou on my right hand, Until I make thy foes thy footstool***" (Acts 2:33-35).

The Progressive Dispensationalists put the cart before the horse because they fail to understand that Psalm 110 reveals that the Lord Jesus had not yet struck through the kings in His day of wrath and therefore He has not yet started to reign from the throne of David. If Peter wanted to tell his listeners that the Lord Jesus is now sitting on the throne of David then he would not have quoted any part of Psalm 110 because that psalm denies that the Lord Jesus is now on the throne of David.

3. The Invisible Kingdom

According to Bock an invisible kingdom began when the Lord Jesus ascended into heaven and it is only invisible because His rule does not originate visibly from the earth:

"*Jesus rules from heaven, not earth, and thus the kingdom is invisible only in the sense that the rule does not originate visibly from earth....Jesus' resurrection-ascension to God's right hand is put forward by Peter as a fulfillment of the Davidic*

70

covenant..." [6]

Beginning at the time when the Lord ascended into heaven an invisible kingdom began, according to Bock. Peter and the rest of the Apostles were with the Lord Jesus Christ for forty days prior to His ascension into heaven while He tutored them about the things concerning the kingdom (Acts 1:3). So if Bock is right about this invisible kingdom then the Lord Jesus would have told them that when He ascended into heaven that He was going to sit upon the throne of David and begin to reign in an invisible kingdom. However, when we consider the question which they asked Him they certainly did not seem to be aware that He was about to initiate this invisible kingdom because they thought it possible that the visible kingdom might be restored to Israel at that time:

"Lord, wilt thou at this time restore again the kingdom to Israel?" (Acts 1:6).

If the Lord Jesus had told them that an invisible kingdom would begin in short order then why did they think that a visible kingdom could be restored at that time? The obvious answer is that He told them nothing about an invisible kingdom which would begin when He ascended into heaven because there is no such thing as an invisible kingdom because the Lord Jesus is not now sitting on the throne of David.

4. A Mystery Form of the Messianic Kingdom?

Craig Blaising quotes the following passage in an

71

effort to try to prove that there is a mystery form of the Messianic Kingdom:

"*The Son of Man will send forth His angels, and they will **gather out of His kingdom** all stumbling blocks, and those who commit lawlessness, and will cast them into the furnace of fire; in that place there shall be weeping and gnashing of teeth. Then the righteous will shine forth as the sun in the kingdom of their Father. He who has ears, let him hear*" (Mt. 13:41-43).

According to Blaising this passage is teaching that the Davidic kingdom will be on the earth before the Lord Jesus returns to the earth because the unsaved will be gathered out of that kingdom. He writes that the words 'gather out of His kingdom' "*would appear to identify a situation 'before' the coming of the Son of Man as 'His kingdom.' Both those who belong to Him and those who will be condemned are present in that form of the kingdom. After His coming, only the saved will be present in the kingdom. Both conditions, before and after His coming are called 'kingdom'...it is not a separate kingdom from that which follows, but a phase, a 'mystery form' of the same kingdom.*" [7]

Blaising is asserting that even before the Lord Jesus returns to the earth (when He will sit upon His throne) the Messianic Kingdom will already be on the earth. If he is right then some of those who will be gathered out of the Messianic Kingdom will be those who are "born again" because only those who are born again can enter into that kingdom (Jn.3:3-

5). So if Blaising is right then we must believe that those who will be born again will be gathered out of the Messianic Kingdom despite the following words of the Lord Jesus:

*"All that the Father giveth me shall come to me; and him that cometh to me **I will in no wise cast out**"* (Jn. 6:37).

The kingdom from which the unsaved will be cast out is the Universal Kingdom which is populated by both the saved and the unsaved:

"The LORD hath prepared his throne in the heavens; and his kingdom ruleth over all" (Ps. 103:19).

There is no such thing as a mystery form of the Messianic Kingdom.

5. Hath Translated Us Into the Kingdom of the Son

Robert Saucy writes that *"the verse that most clearly expresses some kind of present position in the kingdom is Paul's statement that the Father 'has rescued us from the dominion of darkness and brought us into the kingdom of the Son he loves' (Col 1:13)."* [8]

Here is the verse which Saucy quotes:

*"Who hath delivered us from the power of darkness, and **hath translated** us into the kingdom of his dear Son"* (Col. 1:13; KJV).

The Greek word translated "hath translated" means "*to transpose, transfer, remove from one place to another.*" [9]

If anyone belongs to the Messianic kingdom now then there would be no reason why anyone would need to be removed from where they are now to another place. The following is the way that believers have been translated into the kingdom:

"*Even when we were dead in sins, hath quickened us together with Christ, (by grace ye are saved). And hath raised us up together, and made us sit together in heavenly places in Christ Jesus*" (Eph. 2:5-6).

It might be asked why Paul says that Christians have been "*translated us into the kingdom of his dear Son*"?

Paul used that expression because the Christian's life is indeed said to be in the Son:

"*And this is the record, that God hath given to us eternal life, and this life is in his Son*" (1 Jn. 5:11).

At another place Paul wrote that Christ is our life and that our life is hid with Him in God (Col. 3:3-4). So it would be very natural for Paul to say that Christians have been translated into the kingdom of His dear Son.

Believers are said to be "in Christ" and are totally identified with Him and since the Lord Jesus is now sitting at the right hand of the throne of the Father

(Rev.3:21) then it can be said that believers are now with Him as He sits at the side of the throne of the Father. Paul's words at Colossians 1:13 have nothing at all to do with anyone being translated into the Messianic Kingdom.

6. Revelation 3:21

Let us examine the following translation of Revelation 3:21:

*"To him that overcometh will I grant to sit with me **in** my throne, even as I also overcame, and am set down with my Father **in** his throne"* (Rev. 3:21; KJV).

The problem with this translation is that it makes the Lord Jesus being set down "in" the Father's throne despite the fact that He is actually set down at the right hand side of the Father's throne:

*"We have such an high priest, **who is set on the right hand of the throne of the Majesty in the heavens**"* (Heb. 8:1).

The Greek word translated "in" twice at Revelation 3:21 is a primary preposition denoting the location of the Lord Jesus in relation to the throne of God. One of the meanings of that Greek word in regard to location is "by." Joseph Henry Thayer gives the following definition: *"Locally...of proximity, at, near, **by**...at the right hand: Heb. i. 3; viii. 1; Eph.20."* [emphasis added]. [10]

The following is the correct translation:

*"To him that overcometh will I grant to sit with me **by** my throne, even as I also overcame, and am set down with my Father **by** his throne"* (Rev. 3:21).

The Lord Jesus is now "by" the throne of God, specifically at the right hand side of that throne. The Lord Jesus is not "in" that throne. The overcomers spoken of in this verse are believers (1 Jn.5:4) and they will sit at the side of the throne of the Lord Jesus and will reign with Him on the earth:

*"And hast made us unto our God kings and priests: and **we shall reign on the earth**"* (Rev. 5:10).

Since believers will reign with the Lord Jesus by the side of His throne then His throne must be an earthly throne. And at Revelation 3:21 it is clear that the Lord Jesus is now at the side of the Father's throne in heaven and therefore it is not possible that He is now on His own throne, the throne of David. These facts prove that the Lord Jesus is not now sitting at His own throne but instead is sitting at the right hand of God at the heavenly throne. Next, we will see that the Progressive Dispensationalists argue that the throne of David is actually the Father's throne.

7. Is the Throne of David the Heavenly Throne of God?

In his book *Progressive Dispensationalism* Darrell Blaising quotes Revelation 3:21 and then makes an argument that the throne of David is actually the Father's heavenly throne:

"One verse which is sometimes cited as an exception to the Davidic descriptions of Jesus' present throne is Revelation 3:21, 'He who overcomes, I will grant to him to sit down with Me on My throne, as I also overcame and set down with My Father on His throne.' It is alleged that this verse teaches that Jesus is not sitting on the Davidic throne but the divine throne...It is the 'Root of David' who is sitting on the Father's throne. **But the fact that it is said to be the Father's throne, far from presenting a problem to our interpretation, actually affirms it. For this is one of the ways in which the Old Testament spoke of the throne inherited by the Davidic throne; it is in fact the throne of the Lord"** [*emphasis added*]. [11]

Darrell Bock agrees with Blaising that the Davidic throne is not distinct from the heavenly throne of the Father: "*It is also not correct to argue that Psalm 110 refers to a heavenly throne that is distinct from the Davidic, earthly throne. In the Old Testament, these were equated (1 Chron. 29:23; 2 Chron. 9:8). Neither can one argue that the heavenly throne in Revelation 3 and Acts 2 is not Davidic.*" [12]

Bock says that it cannot be argued that the heavenly throne mentioned at Revelation 3:21 is not the Davidic throne.

The biggest problem about their argument is the fact that the Scriptures reveal that the Lord Jesus is now at the right hand of the throne of God and not on that throne. Besides that, the fourth and fifth chapters of the book of Revelation reveal that only one Person is sitting on the one throne (Rev.4:2) and that is God Almighty. So these facts alone disprove Blaising's and Bock's argument that the throne of David is the Father's throne. Their argument is centered on the fact that the Scriptures do describe the throne of David as being the throne of God. Here are the verses which Blaising and Bock cite in their effort to try to prove that the throne of David is the throne of God in heaven:

*"**Then Solomon sat on the throne of the LORD** as king instead of David his father, and prospered; and all Israel obeyed him"* (1 Chron. 29:23).

*"Blessed be the LORD thy God, which delighted in thee to set thee **on his throne**, to be king for the LORD thy God"* (2 Chron. 9:8).

Nothing said in these verses prove that the throne of David is the same throne as the heavenly, eternal throne of God. Instead, we know that the throne of David is described as belonging to God because all things in heaven and in the earth belong to Him:

*"Thine, O LORD is the greatness, and the power, and the glory, and the victory, and the majesty: **for all that is in the heaven and in the earth is thine**; thine is the kingdom, O LORD, and thou art exalted as head above all"* (1 Chron. 29:11).

The throne of David must belong to the LORD God because only the owner can give that throne to the Lord Jesus. The angel Gabriel told Mary the following about the Lord Jesus:

*"He shall be great, and shall be called the Son of the Highest: and **the Lord God shall give unto him the throne of his father David**: And he shall reign over the house of Jacob for ever; and of his kingdom there shall be no end"* (Lk. 1:32,33).

Besides that, the Lord Jesus clearly distinguishes between His throne and the Father's throne because He refers to one as "My throne" and the other as the Father's throne. How can both Blaising and Bock imagine that the throne of David is the throne of God since God's throne has existed from all eternity while the throne of David didn't even come into existence until the tenth century BCE?

8. John 3:12: Earthly Things and Heavenly Things

Craig Blaising wrote that "***The church is a manifestion of the eschatological kingdom*** *because it is an assembly of peoples whom the Messiah, acting with royal authority, has put into relationship with one another, bound by the inaugurated blessings of peace, righteousness, and justice through the Holy Spirit"* [*emphasis added*]. [13]

The Davidic kingdom pertains to earthly things while the Divine plan toward the Body of Christ pertains to heavenly things so it is impossible that the Body of Christ is a manifestion of the eschatological kingdom. The Divine plan toward Israel consists of earthly things, such as the "land" which the LORD gave to the "nation" of Israel and the "government" of that nation. The Scriptures reveal that the Divine purpose toward Israel is earthly in nature which the Divine purpose toward the Body of Christ is heavenly in nature. When we examine the Nicodemus sermon the Lord Jesus' addressed regeneration in connection to the "nation" of Israel as well as the regeneration of "individuals." He told Nicodemus:

"I tell you the truth, no one can see the kingdom of God unless he is born again" (Jn. 3:3; NIV).

To this Nicodemus asked how he could be born again when he is old, and the Lord Jesus said: "*I tell you the truth, no one can enter the kingdom of God unless he is born of water and the Spirit. Flesh gives birth to flesh, but the Spirit gives birth to spirit*" (Jn. 3:5-6; NIV).

Previously the Lord had been speaking of an individual's regeneration but He now begins to speak of the nation of Israel's regeneration. The Lord shifts from using the second person "singular" pronoun "you" to the second person "plural":

*"You should not be surprised at my saying, 'You must be born again. **The wind blows wherever it pleases**. You hear its sound, but you cannot tell where it comes from or where it is going. So it is with everyone born of the Spirit*" (Jn.3:7-8; NIV). [14]

Nicodemus still did not understand, asking, *"How can these things be?"*

By the Lord's reply we can understand that Nicodemus should have been aware of some truth in the OT Scriptures which spoke of a regeneration by the Spirit: "*Art thou a teacher of Israel, and knoweth not these things?*" (v.10).

Sir Robert Anderson writes, "*Here we must keep prominently in view that the truth involved ought to have been known to Nicodemus. 'Art thou the teacher of Israel, and knowest not these things?' the Lord exclaimed in indignant wonder at his ignorance. Therefore in speaking of the new birth by water and the Spirit the Lord referred to some distinctive truth of the Old Testament Scriptures, which ought to have been familiar to a Rabbi of the Sanhedrin.*" [15]

In *The Bible Knowledge Commentary* Edwin A. Blum wrote: "*Nicodemus asked...how this spiritual transformation takes place. Jesus answered that Nicodemus, as the teacher of Israel (the Gr. has the article 'the'), ought to know. The Old Testament prophets spoke of the new Age with its working of the Spirit (Isa.32:15; Ezek.36:25-27; Joel 2:28-29). The nation's outstanding teacher ought to understand how God by His sovereign grace can give someone a new heart.*" [16]

Let us look at one of the passages which Blum cited which does speak of the water and the spirit:

"*Then will **I sprinkle clean water upon you, and ye shall be clean**: from all your filthiness, and from all your idols, will I cleanse you. A new heart also will I give you, and **a new spirit will I put within you**: and I will take away the stony heart out of*

81

your flesh, and I will give you an heart of flesh. And
***I will put my spirit within you**, and cause you to
walk in my statutes, and ye shall keep my
judgments, and do them*"(Ezek. 36:25-27).

Nicodemus should have been aware of that
prophecy as well as the prophecy found in the very
next chapter of the book of Ezekiel that foretells of
the corporate regeneration of Israel. There we see
the prophet taken to a valley full of "dry bones" and
these bones are described as "the whole house of
Israel":

"*The hand of the LORD was upon me, and
carried me out in the spirit of the LORD, and set me
down in the midst of the valley which was full of
bones...Then he said unto me, Son of man, **these
bones are the whole house of Israel**: behold, they
say, Our bones are dried, and our hope is lost: we
are cut off for our parts*" (Ez. 37:1,11).

Charles H. Dyer says, "*To what did this vision
refer? God said it was about **the nation of Israel
(the whole house of Israel)** that was then in
captivity*" [*emphasis added*]. [17]

Then in the verses which follow we see the two
elements which will be instrumental for the future
corporate regeneration of Israel:

"*Again he said to me, "Prophesy to these bones,
and say to them, O dry bones, **hear the word of the
LORD**. Thus says the Lord GOD to these bones:
Behold, **I will cause spirit to enter you, and you
shall live**" (Ezek. 37:4-5; RSVCE).

82

Here Sir Robert Anderson explains the "typical" teaching of the prophecy of the dry bones and how it relates to the teaching of the Lord Jesus to Nicodemus:

"How can sinners, helpless, hopeless, dead - as dead as dry bones scattered upon the earth - be born again to God. "Can these bones live?" is the question of Ezekiel 37: And the answer comes "Prophesy unto these bones, and say unto them, O ye dry bones, hear the word of the Lord.' Preach to dead, lost sinners call upon them to hear the word of the Lord. This is man's part. Or if there be anything more, it is, 'Prophesy unto the Breath. Pray that the Spirit may breathe upon these slain that they may live.' The rest is God's work altogether, for 'the Spirit breathes where He wills.' Not that there is anything arbitrary in His working. God is never arbitrary; but He is always Sovereign. Men preach; the Spirit breathes; and the dry bones live. Thus it is that sinners are born again to God." [18]

Now we will look at "**Heavenly Things**":

Because Nicodemus was ignorant of these prophetic passages that speak of the corporate regeneration of Israel under her New *Diathēkē* the Lord said the following to him:

*"I have spoken to you of **earthly things** and you do not believe; how then will you believe if I speak of **heavenly things**?"* (Jn. 3:12; NIV).

The "earthly things" to which the Lord refers is

the regeneration of the "nation" of Israel. The "heavenly things" are in regard to the blessings received by those in the Body of Christ.

Lewis Sperry Chafer wrote that "*Every covenant, promise, and provisions for Israel is earthly...every covenant or promise for the church is for a heavenly reality, and she continues in heavenly citizenship when the heavens are recreated.*" [19]

Since those in the Body of Christ are "born of God" their citizenship is in heaven:

"*But **our citizenship is in heaven**. And we eagerly await a Savior from there, the Lord Jesus Christ...*" (Phil. 3:20; NIV).

Believers are told that they have been raised up with Christ and are sitting with Him in heavenly places:

"*Even when we were dead in sins, hath quickened us together with Christ, (by grace ye are saved) And **hath raised us up together, and made us sit together in heavenly places in Christ Jesus**"* (Eph. 2:5-6).

How is it possible that the "New Covenant" promised to the nation of Israel can have any efficiency in regard to those with an heavenly citizenship since that covenant is in regard to earthly things? The simple answer is that it can't.

These facts demonstrate that the things in regard to the nation of Israel are in regard to earthly things while the things within the Church parenthesis are in regard to heavenly things.

9. Complementary Hermeneutics and Progressive Dispensationalism

Andrew Woods, who does not agree with the teaching of the Progressive Dispensationalists, writes that *"arguing that Jesus' present position at the Father's right hand represents the Davidic Covenant's fulfillment of any kind is to depart from normal definitions of progress of revelation and consistent, literal or normal, grammatical, historical hermeneutics...**it is only possible to transfer David's throne from earth to heaven in the the Progressive Dispensational system if one embraces 'a priori' a new hermeneutical methodology known as 'complementary hermeneutics'"** [emphasis added].* [20]

The following words of the Progressive Dispensationalists define their new method of interpreting the Scriptures:

*"...does the New Testament 'complement' Old Testament revelation? According to this approach, the New Testament does introduce change and advance; **it does not merely repeat Old Testament revelation. In making complementary additions, however, it does not jettison old promises. The enhancement is not at the expense of the original promise"** [emphasis added].* [21]

The "original promise" regarding the Davidic Covenant was that David's earthly throne was

85

established for ever so it will never be anything other than an earthly throne. And the LORD said that He would not "alter" the promises which He made to David.

Despite these facts the "complementary hermeneutics" used by the Progressives was responsible for their mistaken teaching that the Lord Jesus is now sitting on the throne of David. This method of interpreting the Scriptures does indeed jettison Old Testament promises which the LORD God promised to David which reveal that his throne will always be an earthly throne.

I tend to agree with Andrew Woods' opinion that the Progressive Dispensationalists' complementary hermeneutics "*is in actuality a theology masquerading as a bona fide hermeneutic. In fact, rather than emanating naturally from the biblical text, the ambition to bridge the theological divide between the Dispensational and the Reformed camps appears to be the primary inducement for 'discovering' the notion of a 'complementary hermeneutic,' which comprises the basis of the Progressive Dispensational system.*" [22]

10. Already and Not Yet

Darrell Bock offers the following on the concept of "Already and Not Yet," a concept which is essential to defending the scheme of Progressive Dispensationalism:

"*One should not fear 'already and not yet' terminology, since all Bible students accept its*

86

presence in soteriology: 'I am saved (i.e. justified) already--but I am not yet saved (i.e. glorified) is good theology. The same structure applies to Christology that is wedded to eschatology." [23]

Do all Bible students accept the idea of "already and not yet" when it comes to a person's salvation? The Scriptures refer to the salvation of the soul which happens upon belief (1 Pet.1:9). There is no such thing as an "already/not yet" concept in regard to this kind of salvation. That salvation happens upon belief and it does not happen before a person believes and it does not happen after a person believes. So when we examine a "specific" instance of salvation we see that the idea of an "already/not yet" salvation is not true.

The same can be said about the "kingdom" teaching found in the Bible. The Scriptures speak of the Messianic kingdom which people in their flesh and blood bodies will enter. Then later the same people who will enter this kingdom will also enter the eternal kingdom, a kingdom which people in their flesh and blood bodies cannot enter (1 Cor.15:50). So in a sense, when we combine the two different kingdoms the concept of "already/not yet" can be seen. However, in this discussion the subject is a "specific" kingdom, that being the Messianic kingdom. That kingdom will not come into existence until the Lord Jesus sits upon the throne of David and that will not happen until He returns to the earth. It will not come into existence prior to that so there is no such thing as a Messianic kingdom which begins prior to Him sitting upon that throne. When Paul preached to the Jews he reasoned with them out of the Scriptures:

"And Paul, as his manner was, went in unto them, and three sabbath days **reasoned with them out of the scriptures***"* (Acts 17:2).

In order to accept the idea of a "already/not yet" teaching in regard to the Messianic kingom we must throw our reason to the wind.

End Notes

1. Darrell L. Bock, *Dispensationalism, Israel and the Church*, 43,47.

2. *Ibid.*, 51.

3. *The Companion Bible; King James Version* (Grand Rapids: Kregel, 1990), Appendix 6: "Figures of Speech."

4. Robert L. Saucy, *The Case For Progressive Dispensationalism*, 72.

5. Darrell L. Bock, *Dispensationalism, Israel and the Church*, 62.

6. *Ibid.*, 49,53.

7. Craig A. Blaising, *Progressive Dispensationalism*, 252-53.

8. Robert L. Saucy, *The Case for Progressive Dispensationalism*, 107-8.

9. Joseph Henry Thayer, *A Greek-English Lexicon of the New Testament*, 395.

10. Joseph Henry Thayer, *A Greek-English Lexicon of the New Testament*, 209.

11. Craig A.Blaising, *Progressive Dispensationalism*, 183.

12. Darrell Bock, *Dispensationalism, Israel and the Church*, 63.

13. Craig A. Blaising, *Progressive Dispensationalism*, 287.

14. A footnote in the NIV at verse seven says, "*The Greek is plural.*"

15. Sir Robert Anderson, *The Bible or the Church?* 224.

16. Edwin A. Blum, " John" in *The Bible Knowledge Commentary; New Testament*, 281.

17. Charles H. Dyer, "Ezekiel" in *The Bible Knowledge Commentary; Old Testament*, 1298.

18. Sir Robert Anderson, *Redemption Truths* (Grand Rapids: Kregel Publications, 1980), 137-38.

19. Lewis Spery Chafer, *Systematic Theology*, 4:47.

20. Andrew M. Woods, *The Coming Kingdom* (Duluth, MN: Grace Gospel Press, 2016), 245-6.

21. Craig A. Blaising and Darrell L. Bock,

Dispensationalism, Israel and the Church, 392-3.

22. Andrew M. Woods, *The Coming Kingdom*, 247.

23. Darrell L. Bock, *Dispensationalism, Israel and the Church*, 46.

Chapter IV

Conclusion

The teaching that the Messianic kingdom already exists invariably leads to teaching doctrine which is foreign to the Scriptures. Andrew Woods writes that *"seeing the church as the kingdom causes the church to substitute social causes in lieu of preaching the true gospel...This philosophy and misguided emphasis is known as the 'Social Gospel.' Note this emphasis in the writings of progressive dispensationalists and 'kingdom now' theologian Craig Blaising, who laments, 'Unfortunately, present-day dispensationalists have written very little in proposing a theology of social ministry.' He continues, 'if we as a community of Christ worked on creating our community as a model of social justice and peace, then we really would have some suggestions to make for social reform in our cities and nations."* [1]

In his book *Progressive Dispensationalism* Craig Blaising speaks of another form of evangelicalism which is not found in Traditional Dispensationalism:

*"Its major distinctive is found in its conception of the progressive accomplishment and revelation of **a holistic and unified redemption**. That redemption covers personal, **communal, social, political, and national aspects** of human life...**Another form of***

91

*evangelicalism contributes toward building better
social structures in the larger society* along with
the Gospel message of individual salvation"
[emphasis added]. [2]

Teach No Different Doctrine

Today there are many people within Christendom
who are "*speaking perverse things to draw away
disciples after them*" (Acts 20:30). The following
words of Paul provide help to the sincere believer in
regard to these perverse things:

"*As I urged you when I was going to Macedonia,
remain at Ephesus so that you may charge certain
persons* **not to teach any different doctrine**, *nor to
devote themselves to myths and endless
genealogies, which promote speculations* **rather
than the stewardship from God that is by faith**" (1
Tim.1:3-4; ESV).

Paul warns us away from doctrines which are not
found in his teaching and he makes it plain that the
Christian's true calling is in regard to the following
"stewardship" from God:

"*Each of you should use whatever gift you have
received to serve others,* **as faithful stewards of
God's grace in its various forms**" (1 Pet. 4:10;
NIV).

Among other things the stewardship of which
Peter speaks is the following stewardship which
was given to Paul:

*"For this reason I, Paul, a prisoner of Christ Jesus on behalf of you Gentiles--assuming that you have heard of **the stewardship of God's grace** that was given to me for you"* (Eph. 2:1-2).

This stewardship is in regard to the ministry which Paul speaks of here:

*"But none of these things move me, neither count I my life dear unto myself, so that I might finish my course with joy, and **the ministry**, which I have received of the Lord Jesus, **to testify the gospel of the grace of God**"* (Acts 20: 24).

The Kingdom Which Will Devour the Whole Earth

When the Progressive Dispensationalists teach that the Messianic kingdom has already arrived they overlook the following kingdom found in the book of Daniel:

"The fourth beast shall be the fourth kingdom upon earth, which shall be diverse from all kingdoms, and shall devour the whole earth, and shall tread it down, and break it in pieces" (Dan. 7:23).

Woods addresses that kingdom, writing that *"the next kingdom on the horizon is not the kingdom of God but rather the Antichrist's kingdom. Only after the Antichrist's evil kingdom is personally overthrown by Christ will the Messianic kingdom become an earthly reality. The basic divinely revealed chronology logically teaches that those*

93

*involved in kingdom building in the present Church
Age are not contributing to God's kingdom since
God's kingdom can only come after the Antichrist's
kingdom has been abolished by God. Rather, they
are helping build the next kingdom on the prophetic
horizon, which is the Antichrist's kingdom!"* [3]

The teaching that Christians are now living in the
kingdom will invariably lead to confusion regarding
God's purpose for the Church. This confusion is
addressed by Clarence Larkin in the following way:

*"The 'Kingdom Idea' has robbed the Church of
her 'UPWARD LOOK,' and the 'BLESSED HOPE.'
There cannot be any 'Imminent Coming' to those
who are seeking to 'set up the Kingdom.' The
'Kingdom Idea' has robbed the Church of the
'Pilgrim' and 'Martyr Spirit,' and caused it to go
down into Egypt for help. When the church enters
into an 'Alliance with the World,' and seeks the help
of Parliments, Congresses, Legislatures,
Federations and Reform Societies, largely made up
of ungodly men and women, she loses her
'SPIRITUAL POWER' and becomes helpless as a
redeeming force. The end of such an 'Alliance' will
be a 'Religious Political Regime' that will pave the
way for the revelation of Satan's great 'Religious
Political Leader' and 'Superman'--the
ANTICHRIST."* [4]

The Progressive Dispensationalists fail to
understand that the Body of Christ is not here to
change what Paul calls the present "evil age" into an
age which is righteous. Instead, the Body is here to

94

save perishing souls from the present evil age. The Lord Jesus prayed to the Father about His flock, saying "*I have given them thy word; and the world hath hated them, because **they are not of the world**, even as I am not of the world*" (Jn. 17:14).

Edwin Blum wrote that the disciples "*were in danger because the satanic **world** system **hated them** because **are not** a part of it.*" [5]

The Progressive Dispensationalists seem unaware of these facts and instead have strived to find a way to unite Covenant Theology with Dispensational Theology. And it appears that is the goal of those who decided to allow Progressive Dispensationalism to be taught at Dallas Theological Seminary despite the fact that teaching goes against the Doctrinal Statement of that seminary:

"*We believe that three of these dispensations or rules of life are the subject of extended revelation in the Scriptures, viz., the dispensation of the Mosaic Law, **the present dispensation of grace, and the future dispensation of the millennial kingdom. We believe that these are distinct and are not to be intermingled or confused**, as they are chronologically successive*" [emphasis added]. [6]

The teaching of the Progressive Dispensationalism does indeed intermingle the Church of the present dispensation with the future dispensation of the millennial kingdom, as witnessed by the following words of Craig Blaising:

95

*"**The church is a manifestion of the eschatological kingdom** because it is an assembly of peoples whom the Messiah, acting with royal authority, has put into relationship with one another, bound by the inaugurated blessings of peace, righteousness, and justice through the Holy Spirit"* [emphasis added]. [7]

Now students at Dallas Theological Seminary are taught things which directly contradict the teaching upon which that seminary was founded. In the first chapter of this book overwhelming Scriptual evidence has been presented which demonstrates that the Lord Jesus is not now sitting on the throne of David and therefore the Messianic kingdom is not now in existence. Teaching which contradict the Scriptures was likened to "leaven" or yeast by the Lord Jesus (Mt.16:6-12). Once yeast is added to the dough and the process of leavening begins it continues until the whole lump of dough is leavened:

"A little leaven leaveneth the whole lump" (Gal. 5:9).

That is happening now at Dallas Theological Seminary, as witnessed by the following words of Robert Lightner, who was previously a professor there for many years:

"What concerns me, and a host of others, are some of the things that have been tolerated, are being tolerated and, in fact, promoted by some faculty members. We are fearful of the future. We

96

*are afraid of the long, slippery slope and of what
will happen. We have that fear, not just out of
emotionalism, but out of a reflection on history.
This is exactly what has happened in other
organizations and institutions. There are no sudden
landslides in the Christian community, even in a
Christian's life. Instead, there is always a gradual
trickling and slipping away of the foundation,
picking at the foundation until eventually there is
nothing worthwhile left."* [8]

False teaching feeds on itself and the results will
inevitably be more false teaching. H. Wayne House,
also previously a professor at Dallas Theological
Seminary, had this to say about this subject:

*"One of my best students, and a research
assistant to me at DTS, had told me in the mid-
1990's that he had accepted progressive
dispensationalism. My next meeting with him at the
Dallas Seminary bookstore just two years ago I
discovered that he had embraced amillennialism
and covenant theology. When I asked him about
this he commented to me that it was an easy move
to make from progressive dispensationalism to
amillennialism."* [9]

The fact that Progressive Dispensationalism is
now being taught at DTS is a huge problem and in
the following passage Paul tells us how to solve the
problem:

*"Purge out therefore the old leaven, that ye may
be a new lump"* (1 Cor. 5:7).

97

Paul also tells us how to do that:

*"Preach the word; be instant in season, out of season; reprove, rebuke, **exhort with all longsuffering and doctrine**. For the time will come when they will not endure sound doctrine; but after their own lusts shall they heap to themselves teachers, having itching ears; And they shall turn away their ears from the truth, and shall be turned unto fables. But watch thou in all things, endure afflictions, do the work of an evangelist, make full proof of thy ministry"* (2 Tim.4:2-5).

Sir Robert Anderson wrote that *"Holy Scripture has long been like an elaborate mosaic, of which the several parts have been disturbed, and the main design forgotten. But its hidden harmony was brought to light by the study of 'dispensational truth.'"* [10]

The teaching of Progressive Dispensationalism is an assault on the hidden harmony of the Bible and should no longer be welcome at any institution which teaches dispensational truth.

End Notes

1. Andrew M. Woods, *The Coming Kingdom*, 345.

2. Blaising & Bock, *Progressive Dispensationalism*, 56, 288.

3. Andrew M. Woods, *The Coming Kingdom*, 363-64.

4. Clarence Larkin, *The Second Coming of Christ* (Glenside,PA: Clarence Larkin Estate, 1918), 51.

5. Edwin A. Blum, *The Bible Knowledge Commentary; New Testament*, 332).

6. *Dallas Theological Seminary Doctrinal Statement*, "Article V--The Dispensations" Accessed June 20, 2018. https://www.dts.edu/about/doctrinalstatement/.

7. Craig A. Blaising, *Progressive Dispensationalism*, 287.

8. Robert Lightner, "Progressive Dispensationalism," *Conservative Theological Journal*, Vol. 4, No. 11, March 2000.

9. H. Wayne House, "Dangers of Progressive Dispensationalism to Pre-Millennial Theology," *Pre-Trib. CD 2003*, 3.

10. Sir Robert Anderson, *Unfulfilled Prophecy* (London: Chas. J. Thynne, 1917), 50.

Appendix #1: Defining the Greek Word *Diathēkē*

In order to understand the relationship between the Body of Christ and the New Covenant promised to Israel it is necessary to understand the meaning of the Greek word *diathēkē* which is translated "covenant" in the following verse:

"*For finding fault with them, he saith, Behold, the days come, saith the Lord, when I will make a* **new covenant (diathēkē)** *with the house of Israel and with the house of Judah*" (Heb. 8:8; KJV).

Now let us look at this verse where the word *diathēkē* is used as a promise which God made to Abraham:

"*That we should be saved from our enemies, and from the hand of all that hate us; To perform the mercy promised to our fathers, and to remember* **his holy covenant (diathēkē); The oath** *which he sware to our father Abraham*" (Lk. 1:71-73).

Geerhardus Vos wrote "*in the Gospel i. 72* **the 'diathēkē' is equivalent to the promise given to the fathers; the parallelism in which it stands with the 'oath' of God proves this**: *'to remember his holy 'diathēkē,' the oath which He swore unto Abraham, our father*'" [emphasis added]. [1]

Therefore, we can understand that the Greek word *diathēkē* can mean a "promise."

Let us now look at the following translation of

Jeremiah 31:31 to see that the the Hebrew word translated "covenant" at Jeremiah 31:31 is *berith*:

> "*Behold, the days come, saith the LORD, that I will make a new **covenant (berith)** with the house of Israel, and with the house of Judah*" (Jer. 31:31).

Louis Berkhof wrote that "*In the Septuagint the word 'berith' is rendered 'diathēkē' in every passage where it occurs with the exception of Deut. 9:15 ('marturion') and I Kings 11:11 ('entole'). The word 'diathēkē' is confined to this usage, except in four passages.* **This use of the word seems rather peculiar in view of the fact that it is not the usual Greek word for covenant, but really denotes a disposition, and consequently also a testament. The ordinary word for covenant is 'suntheke'*"* [*emphasis added*]. [2]

According to Berkhof the Greek word *diathēkē* denotes a "disposition" as well as a "testament." In the *The Vocabulary of the Greek Testament* we read that the word *diathēkē* "*is properly 'dispositio,' an 'arrangement' made by one party with plenary power, which the other party may accept or reject, but cannot alter.*" [3]

Here we see that the translators of the Greek Old Testament (LXX) used the Greek word *diathēkē* to translate the Hebrew word *berith*:

> "*Behold, the days come, saith the LORD, that I will make **a new covenant (diathēkē)** with the house of Israel, and with the house of Judah*" (Jer. 31:31; LXX).

101

Vos also wrote that the Greek word *diathēkē* can mean "disposition," writing that "*all that they (the translators of the Greek New Testament) wanted out of 'diathēkē' was the emphasis which the word enabled them to throw upon the one-sided initiative and the unimpaired sovereignty of God in originating the order of redemption..Their procedure appears intelligent only on the supposition that **they believed 'diathēkē' capable of retaining or reacquiring the sense of 'disposition.'**"
4

Now let us look at the following verse:

"*That at that time ye were without Christ, being aliens from the commonwealth of Israel, and strangers from the **covenants (diathēkē) of promise**, having no hope, and without God in the world*" (Eph. 2:12).

In his commentary on this verse Vos says that "*in Eph. ii. 12 the phrase 'covenants of the promise,' in which the genitive is epexegetical, **yields positive proof that Paul regards the 'diathēkē' as so many successive promissory dispositions of God, not as a series of mutual agreements between God and the people**" [emphasis added]. 5

The word *diathēkē* does not carry with it the sense of a compact or of a mutual agreement between two parties, which is the normal understanding of a covenant. Albert Barnes wrote that "*the writers of the New Testament never meant to represent the transactions between God and man*

102

as a 'compact or covenant' properly so called. They have studiously avoided it...The word which they employ - 'diathēkē' - never means a compact or agreement as between equals." [6]

Even though Robert Saucy is a Progressive Dispensationalist he recognizes that the New *Diathēkē* is essentially a "promise," writing that *"because of its gracious **promissory nature, the new covenant is frequently identified with the covenants of promise**"* [emphasis added]. [7]

J. H. Moulton and G. Milligan say that *diathēkē "is properly 'dispositio,' an 'arrangement' made by one party with plenary power, which the other party may accept or reject, but cannot alter. A 'will' is simply the most conspicuous example of such an instrument, which ultimately monopolized the word just because it suited its differentia so completely"* [emphasis added]. [8]

So we can see that the Greek word *diathēkē* can mean a "Promissory Disposition" and it can also mean a "Last will and Testament."

Additional Notes

In regard to Hebrews 9:16-17 some say that what is written there *"does not correspond to any 'any known form of Hellenistic (or indeed any other) legal practice.' A Hellenistic will was secure and valid when it was written down, witnessed and deposited, not when the testator died."* According to this idea the *diathēkē* mentioned in these verses is not speaking of a Last Will and Testament. Based

103

on his study of the Bible Richard Hiers tells another story:

"One other feature of the law of Deuteronomy 21:15-17 is to be noted first. Verse 16 refers to the day on which a man 'assigns his possessions as an inheritance to his sons.' This verse suggests a process very much like testation, the making of a will. What Deuteronomy 21:15-17 says, in effect, is that a man may not ignore his obligation to provide his first-born son with a double portion just because he dislikes that son's mother. Thus, this law is somewhat similar in purpose to modem statutes that prevent one spouse from 'writing' or 'cutting' the other 'out of' his or her will by providing that the survivor may elect a 'spousal share' in lieu of taking under terms of the will." [9]

No doubt there were legal instruments which were promissory dispositions (*diathēkē*) which provided for a transfer of property while the one who made it remained alive but that type of legal instrument would not be the same kind of *diathēkē* (Last Will and Testament) which was not in effect until the one who made it died.

End Notes

1. Geerhardus Vos, "Hebrews, the Epistle of the Diathēkē," in *The Princeton Theological Review*, Vol. 13, No.4, 1915, 613.

2. Louis Berkhof, *Systematic Theology* (Grand Rapids, 1949), 262-63.

3. J.H. Molton and G. Milligan, *The Vocabulary of the Greek Testament* (Grand Rapids: Eerdmans, 1930), 148.

4. Geerhardus Vos, "Hebrews, the Epistle of the Diathēkē," 604-05.

5. *Ibid.*, 609.

6. Albert Barnes, *Notes on the Bible*, Accessed June 5, 2018. https://www.studylight.org/commentaries/bnb/hebrews-8.html.

7. Robert L. Saucy, *The Case for Progressive Dispensationalism*, 121.

8. J.H. Molton and G. Milligan, *The Vocabulary of the Greek Testament*, 148.

9. Richard H. Hiers, *Transfer of Property by Inheritance and Bequest in Biblical Law and Tradition*, Accessed June 5, 2018. http://scholarship.law.ufl.edu/facultypub.

Appendix #2: Ye Do Shew the Lord's Death Till He Comes

The Apostle Paul used a Greek word in regard to the Lord's appearing that can only mean that His appearing could "occur at any moment":

*"For I reckon that the sufferings of this present time are not worthy to be compared with the glory which shall be revealed in us. For the **earnest expectation (apokaradokia)** of the creature waiteth for the manifestation of the sons of God...And not only they, but ourselves also, which have the firstfruits of the Spirit, even we ourselves groan within ourselves, waiting for the adoption, that is, **the redemption of our body**"* (Ro. 8:18,19,23).

Here Paul is speaking of "the redemption of our body", an event that will happen when the Lord Jesus appears. The Greek word translated "earnest expectation" is *apokaradokia*, and this word means *"to watch with head erect or outstretched...to wait for in suspense."* [1]

The same Greek word *"was used in Greek writings to describe the alert watchman who peered into the darkness, eagerly looking for the first gleam of the distant beacon which would announce the capture of Troy."* [2]

This proves that those in the Body of Christ were not taught to be waiting for the Lord Jesus to appear when He returns to the earth because before that can happen certain events must happen first, such as the setting up of the abomination of desolation in the holy place (Mt.24:15). Paul certainly would not be telling anyone to looking eagerly with their head outstretched for the appearance of the Lord Jesus if He couldn't even appear until the abomination of desolations is first set up in the holy place.

Why the Delay?

Sir Robert Anderson writes the following about the delay: "*How, then, can the lapse of centuries be accounted for? The forty years' sojourn of Israel in the wilderness may suggest the answer. Theirs was a true hope who fled from Egypt, with their faces toward the promised land which lay but a few days' march across the desert; and yet two men alone of all that host ever planted foot upon the soil of Palestine. And why? Because they let slip the hope, and in heart turned back to Egypt. And can any one read the later Epistles, and the Revelation, and fail to mark how closely the Christian Church followed in the footsteps of the Jewish people? Can we wonder, then, that 'the same example of unbelief' should reap the same results? Apostasy on earth, and long-suffering in heaven, afford the true solution of the mystery of long centuries of desert wandering and trial for a Church which, in its pristine purity and life, was called to wait for, and expect with joyful confidence, its absent Lord's return.*" [3]

The Lord's appearance which applies to Christians has nothing at all to do with the Lord Jesus' return to the earth to set up His kingdom.

Instead, Christians are the Lord's ambassadors (2 Cor. 5:20) and before any war the ambassadors are recalled and bought back to their place of citizenship. Since the Christian's citizenship is in heaven (Phil. 3:20) then the LORD God will catch up His saints and bring them to their place of citizenship before the great tribulation.

End Notes

1. Joseph Henry Thayer, *A Greek-English Lexicon of the New Testament*, 62.

2. *Precept Austin*, "Romans 8:18-19 Commentary," Accessed May 16, 2008. http://www.preceptaustin.org/romans_818-39.

3. Sir Robert Anderson, *The Way* (London: James Nesbet & Co., Limited, 1905), 120-121.

Appendix #3: The Chronology of the End Times

Let us now examine the chronology for the end times events. As already shown in Appendix #2, the Lord can appear at any moment and the living saints will be caught up to meet the Lord in the air and at that time all of the members of the Body, both dead and alive, will put on glorious bodies like that of the Lord Jesus.

Next, let us look about what is said in the following passage about the Lord Jesus' return to the earth:

"Which also said, Ye men of Galilee, why stand ye gazing up into heaven? this same Jesus, which is taken up from you into heaven, **shall so come in like manner as ye have seen him go into heaven.** *Then returned they unto Jerusalem from* **the mount called Olivet***, which is from Jerusalem a sabbath day's journey"* (Acts 1:11-12).

In his commentary on these verse S. Lewis Johnson wrote, *"And so how will Jesus come again? Well, look at it for a moment and think about it. He went up personally. He will come back personally. He went up in bodily form --glorified bodily form, but bodily form. He will come back in glorified bodily form. He went up in visible form. He will come back in visible form.* **He went up from a particular place, the Mount of Olives. He will come back --Zechariah tells us--to a** *particular place, the Mount of Olives"* [*emphasis added*]. [1]

Yes, when the Lord Jesus returns to the earth He will fulfill the following prophecy of Zechariah and in that day His feet shall stand on the Mount of Olives:

"For I will gather all nations against Jerusalem to battle; and the city shall be taken, and the houses rifled, and the women ravished; and half of the city shall go forth into captivity, and the residue of the people shall not be cut off from the city. ***Then shall the LORD go forth, and fight against those nations, as when he fought in the day of battle. And his feet shall stand in that day upon the mount of Olives****, which is before Jerusalem on the east"* (Zech. 14:2-4).

John Walvoord wrote that *"**The great tribulation**...is a specific period of time beginning with the abomination of desolation **and closing with the second coming of Christ**"* [*emphasis added*] [2]

Yes, the Lord Jesus will return at the end of the great tribulation and rescue His people at the time of their greatest peril. Let us look at the events leading up to the the great tribulation:

*"When ye therefore shall see **the abomination of desolation**, spoken of by Daniel the prophet, stand in the holy place...Then let them which be in Judaea flee into the mountains...But pray ye that your flight be not in the winter, neither on the sabbath day:*

110

*For then shall be **great tribulation**, such as was not since the beginning of the world to this time, no, nor ever shall be. **And except those days should be shortened, there should no flesh be saved: but for the elect's sake those days shall be shortened**"* (Mt. 24:15-22).

First the abomination of desolation will stand in the holy place and then "there shall be great tribulation." Then we read that the tribulation will be shortened and that will happen when the Lord Jesus returns to the earth and fights against all the nations which will come against Jerusalem (Zech.14:1-3). This is the only place in the Lord's timeline where the prophecy of Zechariah 14:1-4 can be fulfilled because it takes place before the Lord Jesus begins to reign as King (Zech.14:9).

However, when we look at the same timeline outlined by the Lord Jesus concerning these events it appears that the Lord Jesus will not return until AFTER the great tribulation:

*"**But immediately after the tribulation of those days the sun shall be darkened**, and the moon shall not give her light, and the stars shall fall from heaven, and the powers of the heavens shall be shaken:and then **the sign of the Son of Man will appear in the sky. Then all the tribes of the earth will mourn, and they will see the Son of Man coming on the clouds of the sky** with power and great glory"* (Mt. 24:29-30).

How can this be reconciled with the fact that the

Lord Jesus will return at the end of the great tribulation and not until after the great tribulation is over? When the Lord spoke of the "sign" of the Son of Man appearing in the sky at Matthew 24:30 His words were in answer to the disciple's question concerning the "sign" of His coming:

*"As Jesus was sitting on the Mount of Olives, the disciples came to him privately. 'Tell us,' they said, 'when will this happen, and what will be **the sign of your coming** and of the end of the age"'* (Mt. 24:3; NIV).

Therefore, we can understand that when all of the tribes of the earth see Him in the sky that will be a "sign" of His coming and not His actual coming to the earth. In *The Bible Knowledge Commentary* Louis Barbieri, Jr., wrote: *"Exactly what the sign of the Son of Man will be is unknown...the sign may be the lightening, **or perhaps the Lord Himself**"* [*emphasis added*]. [3]

Now let us look at the following verse again:

*"**But immediately after the tribulation of those days the sun shall be darkened, and the moon shall not give her light, and the stars shall fall from heaven, and the powers of the heavens shall be shaken:and then the sign of the Son of Man will appear in the sky.** Then all the tribes of the earth will mourn, and they will see the Son of Man coming on the clouds of the sky with power and great glory"* (Mt. 24:29-30).

According to this passage the Lord Jesus will be

seen in the sky after the sun and the moon will be darkened. The following verse speaks of those same signs and the same appearance of the Lord Jesus and from this prophecy we know that He will be departing from Jerusalem when He will be seen in the sky:

"*The sun and the moon shall be darkened, and the stars shall withdraw their shining. The LORD also shall roar out of Zion, and utter his voice from Jerusalem*; *and the heavens and the earth shall shake: but the LORD will be the hope of his people, and the strength of the children of Israel*" (Joel 3:15-16).

So we can know that when the Lord Jesus returns to the earth He will fulfill the prophecy at Zechariah 14 and therefore we know that no one will be caught up when the Lord Jesus descends from heaven. That is because it will not be until after the great tribulation is over and the Lord Jesus roars out of Jerusalem when the saints will be gathered together:

"*But in those days, **after that tribulation**, the sun shall be darkened, and the moon shall not give her light, And the stars of heaven shall fall, and the powers that are in heaven shall be shaken. And then shall they see the Son of man coming in the clouds with great power and glory. **And then shall he send his angels, and shall gather together his elect from the four winds, from the uttermost part of the earth to the uttermost part of heaven***" (Mk.13:24-27).

113

If the saints are caught up to meet the Lord Jesus in the air when He descends from heaven while returning to the earth then there would be no need for the angels to gather together the elect because the elect would have already met the Lord Jesus in the air:

*"Then we which are alive and remain shall be caught up together with them in the clouds, **to meet the Lord in the air**"* (1 Thess. 4:17).

It is impossible that the rapture can happen at the time of the Lord Jesus' return to the earth when His feet shall stand on the Mount of Olives.

Next, let us look at the following things which will happen after the great tribulation is over:

*"And there shall be signs in the sun, and in the moon, and in the stars; and **upon the earth distress of nations, with perplexity; the sea and the waves roaring; Men's hearts failing them for fear, and for looking after those things which are coming on the earth**...for as a snare shall it come **on all them that dwell on the face of the whole earth**""* (Lk. 21:25-26,35).

These events will happen after the great tribulation is over because the signs in the sky spoken of in this passage will happen after the great tribulation is over (Mt. 24:29). The following verses from the book of Revelation speaks about these same things, things which will happen after the signs are seen in the sky:

"And I beheld when he had opened the sixth seal, and, lo, there was a great earthquake; and the sun became black as sackcloth of hair, and the moon became as blood; And the stars of heaven fell unto the earth...And the kings of the earth, and the great men, and the rich men, and the chief captains, and the mighty men, and every bondman, and every free man, hid themselves in the dens and in the rocks of the mountains; And said to the mountains and rocks, Fall on us, and hide us from the face of him that sitteth on the throne, and from the wrath of the Lamb: For the great day of his wrath is come; and who shall be able to stand?...And another angel came out of the temple, crying with a loud voice to him that sat on the cloud, Thrust in thy sickle, and reap: for the time is come for thee to reap; for the harvest of the earth is ripe. And he that sat on the cloud thrust in his sickle on the earth; and the earth was reaped" (Rev. 6:12-17;14:15-16).

After the world wide harvest the Lord will usher in the Messianic kingdom, the kingdom which will be populated by only those who have been born again (Jn. 3:3-5). Being back on the earth those in the Body of Christ will judge the world (1 Cor. 6:2) and the nation of Israel will be restored to her previous position as a special people unto the Lord. Then all those on the earth will enjoy the times of refreshing and the restitution of all things which will come from the presence of the Lord Jesus (Acts 3:19-21). Then after the thousand years are over the universe will be destroyed and the kingdom will enter the eternal state (2 Pet. 3:10-11; Heb. 1:10-11;

1 Cor.15:24). While in flesh and blood bodies people are not equipped to see things belonging to the eternal state (2 Cor. 4:18). But when we will be raised in spiritual bodies (1 Cor. 15:44 i.e. bodies belonging to the spiritual sphere) we will enter into the kingdom of God, the same kingdom of which people in their flesh and blood bodies cannot enter (1 Cor. 15:50). Then we will see the face of God (Rev. 22:4). From this we can understand that things described as being "spiritual" does not mean an absence of substance but instead things belonging to the spiritual, eternal sphere. And here is a vision which John was given of the Lord Jesus while in the spiritual sphere:

"And in the midst of the seven candlesticks one like unto the Son of man, clothed with a garment down to the foot, and girt about the paps with a golden girdle. His head and his hairs were white like wool, as white as snow; and his eyes were as a flame of fire; And his feet like unto fine brass, as if they burned in a furnace; and his voice as the sound of many waters. And he had in his right hand seven stars: and out of his mouth went a sharp twoedged sword: and his countenance was as the sun shineth in his strength. And when I saw him, I fell at his feet as dead" (Rev. 1:13-17).

All those in the Body of Christ will put on bodies just like His glorious body!

End Notes

1. S. Lewis Johnson, *The Plan and the Power*

116

and the Promise, Accessed June 6, 2018.
http://sljinstitute.net/acts/the-plan-the-power-and-
the-promise/

2. John F. Walvoord *The Signs of the End of the Age*, Accessed June 8, 2018.
https://bible.org/seriespage/24-signs-end-age

3. Louis Barbieri, Jr., "Matthew" in *The Bible Knowledge Commentary; NewTestament*, 78.

Appendix #4: The Gospel as the Last Will and Testament of Christ

The Spiritual blessings which are received through the gospel are described in terms of a Last Will and Testament of Christ. Believers of the gospel are "heirs" of that Will and receive an "inheritance" which flow from that Will:

*"That the Gentiles should be **fellowheirs**, and of the same body, and partakers of his promise in Christ **by the gospel**"* (Eph. 3:6).

*"That we should be to the praise of his glory, who first trusted in Christ. In whom ye also trusted, after that ye heard the word of truth, **the gospel of your salvation**: in whom also after that ye believed, ye were sealed with that holy Spirit of promise, Which is the earnest of **our inheritance** until the redemption of the purchased possession, unto the praise of his glory"* (Eph. 1:12-14).

The Gospel of the Grace of God

Next, the following passage speaks of the gospel of grace, the gospel which is the Last Will and Testament of Christ:

*"And now apart from law hath the righteousness of God been manifested, testified to by the law and the prophets, and **this righteousness of God is** through the faithfulness of Jesus Christ **to all, and upon all those who believe**, -- for there is no difference, for all did sin, and are come short of the*

118

*glory of God --**being declared righteous freely by His grace through the redemption that is in Christ Jesus**, whom God did set forth a mercy seat, through the faith in his blood, for the shewing forth of His righteousness, because of the passing over of the bygone sins in the forbearance of God*" (Ro. 3:21-25).

These words spell out the Last Will and Testament of Christ, and as in every will the inheritance is based on the death of the testator. And here the death is spoken of as being "the redemption" which is in Christ Jesus, that believers are redeemed by His blood:

"*Forasmuch as ye know that ye were not **redeemed** with corruptible things, as silver and gold, from your vain conversation received by tradition from your fathers; **But with the precious blood of Christ, as of a lamb without blemish and without spot**" (1 Pet. 1:18-19).

The "inheritance" is the righteousness of God which is apart from law or works of any kind and the "heirs" are believers. And it is all made possible because believers are "*declared righteous freely by His grace through the redemption that is in Christ Jesus.*"

In the following verse Paul speaks about that inheritance and says that it is received by faith:

"*And be found in him, not having mine own righteousness, which is of the law, but that which is through the faithfulness of Christ, **the***

119

righteousness which is of God by faith" (Phil. 3:9).

This is the gospel which Paul preached among the Gentiles and those who heard it and believed it "*knew the grace of God in truth*"(Col. 1:5-6).

In the following passage Paul speaks of Abraham receiving this imputed righteousness of God by faith and says that those in the Body also receive it by faith:

"*He staggered not at the promise of God through unbelief; but was strong in faith, giving glory to God; And being fully persuaded that, what he had promised, he was able also to perform. **And therefore it was imputed to him for righteousness**. Now it was not written for his sake alone, that it was imputed to him; **But for us also, to whom it shall be imputed, if we believe on him that raised up Jesus our Lord from the dead**" (Ro. 4:20-25).

Those who lived under the law at a time before the gospel of grace was preached were saved under the terms of the gospel of grace:

"*For this reason Christ is the mediator of a new testament, that those who are called may receive the promised eternal inheritance--**now that he has died as a ransom to set them free from the sins committed under the first covenant**. In the case of a will, it is necessary to prove the death of the one who made it*" (Heb. 9:15-16).

In order understand how the gospel of grace applied to those who lived before that gospel was preached let us look at the following passage and notice what is in "bold":

*"And now apart from law hath the righteousness of God been manifested, **testified to by the law and the prophets**, and this righteousness of God is through the faithfulness of Jesus Christ to all, and upon all those who believe..."* (Ro. 3:21-22).

When Paul said that this righteousness apart from law is "testified to by the law and the prophets" he is saying that this principle by which people are saved is found in the Old Testament. Then in the next chapter he uses both Abraham and David to illustrate this way of salvation. In Abraham's case, he received the imputed righteousness which is of God when he "believed God" (Ro. 4:3). Here is what he said about David who lived under the law:

"But to him that worketh not, but believeth on him that justifieth the ungodly, his faith is counted for righteousness. Even as David also describeth the blessedness of the man, unto whom God imputeth righteousness without works, Saying, Blessed are they whose iniquities are forgiven, and whose sins are covered. Blessed is the man to whom the Lord will not impute sin" (Ro. 4:5-8).

David was not saved when he believed the gospel of grace because he never heard that gospel. Instead, he was saved under the terms of the gospel of grace, that all those who believe receive the imputed righteousness of God:

"And now apart from law hath the

121

righteousness of God been manifested, *testified to by the law and the prophets, and **this righteousness of God is** through the faithfulness of Jesus Christ **to all, and upon all those who believe***, -- *for there is no difference, for all did sin, and are come short of the glory of God --being declared righteous freely by His grace through the redemption that is in Christ Jesus, whom God did set forth a mercy seat, through the faith in his blood, for the shewing forth of His righteousness*, **because of the passing over of the bygone sins in the forbearance of God**" (Ro. 3:21-25).

The bygone sins of those like David were passed over because his sins were later redeemed by the Lord Jesus at the Cross.

Appendix #5: Understanding the Church Parenthesis

The Scriptures reveal that when the nation of Israel was in a covenant relationship with the LORD the children of Israel were a special people unto Himself:

"*For thou art an holy people unto the LORD thy God: the LORD thy God hath chosen thee to be **a special people unto himself, above all people that are upon the face of the earth**"* (Deut. 7:6).

On the other hand, during the Church age there are no special people unto the LORD except for believers and in the Body of Christ there is no distinction between the Jews and those of other nationalities:

"*And have put on the new man, which is renewed in knowledge after the image of him that created him: **Where there is neither Greek nor Jew, circumcision nor uncircumcision**, Barbarian, Scythian, bond nor free: but Christ is all, and in all"* (Col. 3:10-11).

As I have already pointed out, when the Divine plan toward Israel is in effect then the children of Israel are above all people on the face of the earth so therefore it is impossible that at the same time the Divine plan is also toward the Body of Christ where there is no difference between the Jews and the Gentiles. It is evident that the two different Divine plans are mutually exclusive and, as Lewis

123

Sperry Chafer said, the Divine plan toward the Church is *"unrelated to any divine purpose which precedes it or follows it."* [1]

Earlier I pointed out that the LORD's plan toward Israel is "earthly" in nature while His plan toward the Body of Christ is "heavenly" in nature. This is another example which demostrates that the two Divine plans are mutually exclusive.

1. Daniel's Seventy Weeks

Charles Ryie said that the church parenthesis is seen in Daniel's prophecy about the seventy weeks. *"An intercalation is an insertion of a period of time in a calendar,"* he says, *"and a parenthesis in one sense is defined as an interlude or interval...So either or both words can be appropriately used to define the church age if one sees **a distinct interlude in God's program for Israel (as clearly taught in Daniel's prophecy of the seventy weeks in 9:24-27)**"* [emphasis added]. [2]

The first 69 weeks of the prophecy was fulfilled with the Lord Jesus' death upon the Cross--*"Messiah cut off."* (Dan.9:26). The 70th week remains in the future: *"And he shall confirm the covenant with many for one week: and in the midst of the week he shall cause the sacrifice and the oblation to cease, **and for the overspreading of abominations he shall make it desolate**, even until the consummation, and that determined shall be poured upon the desolate"* (Dan. 9:27).

The abomination of desolations spoken of in this

verse is the same thing spoken of by the Lord Jesus in the following verse and its fulfillment remains in the future:

"*When ye therefore shall see **the abomination of desolation, spoken of by Daniel the prophet**, stand in the holy place, (whoso readeth, let him understand) Then let them which be in Judaea flee into the mountains*" (Mt. 24:15-16).

Andrew Woods writes that "*the first 69 weeks of Daniel's prophecy of the 70 Weeks (Dan. 9:24-27) represent God's past program for national Israel while the 70th week represents God's future program for national Israel. The Church age transpires in the interlude between the 69th and 70th weeks. Thus, the church represents a unique spiritual organization where Jews and Gentiles experience equal status (Eph. 2:11-22) in between God's past and future program for national Israel. This interlude is best captured through the conceptual tool of a parenthesis.*" [3]

The Divine plan toward Israel was in regard to things which were prophesised while the Divine plan toward the Body of Christ was in regard to things which were kept secret. So once again we see that the two Divine plans are mutually exclusive.

2. The Dispensation of the Mystery

In the following verse Paul refers to a "dispensation" or "stewardship" which Christians are given and he refers to it as the "dispensation of the mystery":

*"and to make all men see what is **the dispensation of the mystery** which for ages hath been hid in God who created all things"* (Eph.3:9; ASV).

Christians have been made stewards of this mystery which has been hidden in God:

*"Let a man so account of us, as of the ministers of Christ, **and stewards of the mysteries of God**"* (1 Cor. 4:1).

The reason why this "mystery" was kept secret is because if it had been revealed prior to the Cross then the princes of the world would not have crucified the Lord Jesus Christ:

"But we speak the wisdom of God in a mystery, even the hidden wisdom, which God ordained before the world unto our glory: Which none of the princes of this world knew: for had they known it, they would not have crucified the Lord of glory" (1 Cor. 2:7-8).

Paul refers to this "mystery" as being a "hidden" wisdom, or something which was not previously revealed in the Scriptures. That is the same "mystery" that Christians are to preach to the unsaved:

*"Now to him who is able to establish you in accordance with **my gospel, the message I proclaim about Jesus Christ, in keeping with the revelation of the mystery hidden for long ages past**, but now revealed and made known through*

126

*the prophetic writings by the command of the eternal God, **so that all the Gentiles might come to the obedience that comes from faith**"* (Ro. 16:25-26; NIV).

The only "mystery" which Christians are to preach to the unsaved is the truth found in the gospel, that believers are *"justified freely by his grace through the redemption that is in Christ Jesus"* (Ro. 3:24).

That truth was not revealed in the OT and that explains Paul's words in "bold" when he speaks the gospel of grace:

*"**But now** apart from the law the righteousness of God **has been made known**, to which the Law and the Prophets testify"* (Ro. 3:21).

The believer is redeemed by the blood of the Lord Jesus (1 Pet. 1:18-19) so it is the death of the Lord Jesus which brings salvation to all who believe. And if the princes of the world would have known that believers are saved by the blood of the Lord Jesus then they wouldn't have crucified him. Now let us look at the following passage:

*"Of which salvation the prophets have enquired and searched diligently, who prophesied of the grace that should come unto you: **Searching what, or what manner of time the Spirit of Christ which was in them did signify, when it testified beforehand the sufferings of Christ**, and the glory that should follow. Unto whom it was revealed, that not unto themselves, but unto us they did minister*

*the things, which are now reported unto you by
them that have preached the gospel unto you with
the Holy Spirit sent down from heaven"* (1 Pet.
1:10-12).

Here Peter is saying that the prophets searched
diligently in an effort to determine what the
prophecies concerning Christ's suffering did signify
but it was not revealed unto them. Even the Twelve
Apostles, those closest to the Lord Jesus, did not
realize that He was going to die (Lk. 18:31-34) or
be resurrected (Jn. 20:9). They certainly did not
know the "purpose" of the Cross, that God hath
made Jesus Christ *"to be sin for us, who knew no
sin; that we might be made the righteousness of
God in him"* (2 Cor. 5:21).

Roger M. Raymer writes the following about
Peter's words which I just quoted: *"Concerning this
salvation (cf. 'salvation' in vv. 5, 9) the
prophets...searched intently and with the greatest
care their own Spirit-guided writings. They longed
to participate in this salvation and coming period of
grace and tried to discover the appointed time and
circumstances to which the Spirit of Christ in them
was pointing.* **They pondered how the glorious
Messiah could be involved in suffering"** [*emphasis
added*]. [4]

The following verse has lead some to believe that
John the Baptist was speaking about what the Lord
Jesus accomplished at the Cross:

"The next day John seeth Jesus coming unto him,

128

and saith, Behold the Lamb of God, **which taketh away the sin of the world**" (Jn. 1:29).

Sir Robert Anderson says the following about that translation:

"This is not translation merely, it savours of exegesis. 'Who beareth the sin of the world' is what the Baptist said. His words were not a prophecy of what Christ would accomplish by His death, but a statement of what He was in His life. Mark the present tense, 'Who is bearing.' And while the word used in 1 Peter 1:2-24, and in kindred passages, is a sacrificial term, we have here an ordinary word for lifting and carrying burdens. When the Lord sighed in healing the deaf mute by the Sea of Galilee, and when He groaned and wept at the grave of Lazarus, He took upon Himself, as it were, the infirmities and sorrows which He relieved, and made them His own. And in this pregnant sense it was that He bore the world's sin. In this sense of the word He was manifested to bear sins, and in no other sense was He a sin-bearer during His earthly life." [5]

Here is the verse from the OT which John the Baptist was referring to at John 1:29:

*"**He bears our sins, and is pained for us**: yet we accounted him to be in trouble, and in suffering, and in affliction"* (Isa. 43:4; LXX).

Since the believer's stewardship responsiblity during the Church age is to preach a truth which was not revealed in the OT then it becomes obvious

129

that the Christian's service in this age has nothing at all to do with any stewardship found in the OT.

3. The Divine Plan Toward Israel as "Type"

In an earlier chapter I demonstrated that when speaking to Nicodemus the Lord Jesus employed a "type" in regard to the future regeneration of the "nation" of Israel to picture or illustrate the "individual's" regeneration. It is widely recognized that the history of the "nation" of Israel in regard to her redemption is a "type" which illustrates or pictures the "antitype," the redemption of the "individual" believer. Now let us look at the following passage where we see the Greek word *typos*, the word translated as "type" in English:

"*Moreover, brethren, I would not that ye should be ignorant, how that all our fathers were under the cloud, and all passed through the sea; And were all baptized unto Moses in the cloud and in the sea; And did all eat the same spiritual meat; And did all drink the same spiritual drink: for they drank of that spiritual Rock that followed them: and that Rock was Christ. But with many of them God was not well pleased: for they were overthrown in the wilderness. Now these things were our examples (typos), to the intent we should not lust after evil things, as they also lusted*" (1 Cor. 10:1-6).

Ada Habershon writes that "*It is very important to understand what is meant by a type. In I Cor. x. we are told concerning the various wilderness experiences of the children of Israel, that 'all these*

130

*things happened unto them for types' ; and **Paul explains that the record of these events is given to us in the Bible for a special purpose, viz., to teach us certain lessons**. This passage seems to cover all that befell God's redeemed people in their journey from the place of bondage to the land of promise ; and **we may also conclude from it that other portions of their history are given to us for a similar purpose**" [emphasis added].* [6]

David realized that the redemption of Israel was a "national" redemption:

"***And what one nation in the earth is like thy people, even like Israel***, *whom God went to redeem for a people to himself...**which thou redeemedst to thee from Egypt**, from the nations and their gods?*" (2 Sam. 7:23).

In a lecture addressed to Dallas Theological Seminary on the subject of Typology Charles Fritsch stated that "*the exodus, **the deliverance of a nation**, becomes a type of the redemptive work of Christ-- also clearly adumbrated in the exile-- **where the individual is brought to realize his own tremendous guilt and need of redemption**" [emphasis added]*. [7]

Henry W. Soltau understands the principle that the "redemption" provided by the passover lambs was "nationalistic" in nature: "*Israel was considered one assembly in redemption through the blood of the Paschal Lamb in Egypt. Though many lambs were slain, ('a lamb for a house,') yet they*

131

were considered as one lamb: 'the whole assembly of the congregation shall kill it in the evening' Exod. Xii. 6." [8]

The New Covenant promised to Israel is corporate in nature and it will be through this covenant that the "nation" of Israel will receive the promised blessings. This is the "type."

On the other hand, all "individual" believers are saved and receive the promise of eternal life through the operation of the Last Will and Testament of Christ, the gospel of Christ:

"For this reason Christ is the mediator of a new testament, that those who are called may receive the promised eternal inheritance--now that he has died as a ransom to set them free from the sins committed under the first covenant" (Heb. 9:15).

Craig A. Blaising writes that "*the heavenly nature of the church's salvation was interpreted by classical dispensationalists in an **individualistic manner**. Political and social issues were 'earthly' matters which did not concern the church. The church was a spiritual unity found in Christ. This unity manifested itself not only in the oneness of Christ but in the oneness of personal salvation. **Issues in the church were individual, private, spiritual matters, not social, political, earthly matters**"* [emphasis added]. [9]

These things reveal that the Divine plan toward Israel can be seen in "types" and these types illustate the "anti-types," the things which are in

132

regard to "individual" believers.

Traditional Dispensationalists Saw This Typological Relationship

Some of the earlier Traditional Dispensationalists saw a typical relationship between the two. In his book *Progressive Dispensationalism* Craig A. Blaising points out that C.I. Scofield taught that the blessing of the Spirit under Israel's New Covenant "**typified**" the blessing of the Spirit that is in regard to the Body of Christ: "*Scofield...interpreted the New Covenant in the same manner as he did the Abrahamic covenant: literally it had to do with God's earthly plan for Israel; spiritually it revealed God's spiritual plan for the church (**the blessing of the Spirit for Israel in Ezekiel 36 typified the church's blessing of the Spirit**)...*" [*emphasis added*]. [10]

Blaising continues, stating that "*Classical dispensationalists believed that the biblical covenants would be fulfilled for earthly people in the Millennium and eternal state. Since the covenants did not concern heavenly people (except in a **typological** or spiritual sense) it was not proper to say that they were being fulfilled in the present dispensation (except in a spiritual or **typological manner**)*" [*emphasis added*]. [11]

The two plans of God are mutually exclusive because the "type" and the "anti-type" are mutually exclusive.

4. The Everlasting Covenant

133

Here we see that the New Covenant promised to Israel is described as being "everlasting":

*"And I will make an **everlasting ('owlam)** **covenant** with them, that I will not turn away from them, to do them good; but I will put my fear in their hearts, that they shall not depart from me"* (Jer. 32:40).

Here the Hebrew word *'owlam* is translated "everlasting" and that word does not always refer to endless time. When that word is used as referring to the future, as at Jeremiah 32:40, then the meaning of that word is *"defined by the nature of the thing itself"*: *"It more often refers to 'future time,' in such a manner, that what is called 'terminus ad quem,' it is always defined by the nature of the thing itself"* (*Geseniu's Lexicon*).

The context in which the word *'owlam* is found determines the length of the "age" to which it refers. For instance, consider the following verse:

*"And if the servant shall plainly say, I love my master, my wife, and my children; I will not go out free: Then his master shall bring him unto the judges; he shall also bring him to the door, or unto the door post; and his master shall bore his ear through with an aul; and he shall serve him **for ever ('owlam)**"* (Ex. 21:5-6).

Here it is said that if a servant desires to stay with his master for the rest of his life then "he shall serve him for ever." By the context we can understand that the servent will not serve his master for eternity or for an endless amount of time but instead for the remainder of his life.

In order to illustrate this principle let us look at what is said in regard to the land that God gave to Jacob:

*"And **they shall dwell in the land that I have given unto Jacob** my servant, wherein your fathers have dwell...**My tabernacle also shall be with them**: yea, I will be their God, and they shall be my people. And the heathen shall know that I the LORD do sanctify Israel, **when my sanctuary shall be in the midst of them for evermore (`owlam)**"* (Ez. 37:25-28).

It is not possible that the Lord will shall be in the midst of them throughout eternity since the land which God gave Jacob is going to be destroyed at some time in the future:

*"But the day of the Lord will come as a thief in the night; in the which **the heavens shall pass away with a great noise, and the elements shall melt with fervent heat, the earth also and the works that are therein shall be burned up**. Seeing then that **all these things shall be dissolved**...Nevertheless we, according to his promise, look for new heavens and a new earth, wherein dwelleth righteousness"* (2 Pet. 3:10-11, 13).

*"And, Thou, Lord, in the beginning hast laid the foundation of the earth; and the heavens are the works of thine hands: **They shall perish**; but thou*

remainest" (Heb. 1:10-11).

Of course that will not happen until after the Millennium is over and that kingdom is delivered up to the Father in the eternal state:

"*Then cometh the end, when he shall have delivered up the kingdom to God, even the Father; when he shall have put down all rule and all authority and power*" (1 Cor. 15:24).

Craig A Blaising acknowledges that both Charles Ryrie and John Walvoord believe that the "everlasting" promises in regard to things in the "earthly" sphere will come to an end. He says that both these men "*claim that promises about an earthly kingdom forever do not really mean 'forever.' Or, they say that they only apply to time and history such that when time and history have come to an end and give way to a timeless eternity, then the 'everlasting' promises, which only apply to time and history, will be considered as having been fulfilled.*" [12]

Blaising continues, writing that "*at the end of the Millennium, Walvoord sees the earthly (Davidic) kingdom coming to an end. The universal and spiritual kingdoms will be united forever. Although he sometimes uses the new earth language of Revelation 21, Walvoord makes a radical distinction between the millennial and eternal states. He does not relate the everlasting promises of Old Testament hope to this eternal state, but sees them fulfilled in the Millennium. In fact, Walvoord*

136

is insistent that they 'cannot' be fulfilled on the new earth. This is due to the 'radical differences' between the two states, such that the latter does not possess the conditions for the fulfillment of these promises." [13]

The believer's final state will be in heaven because that is the place of His citizenship:

*"But **our citizenship is in heaven**. And we eagerly await a Savior from there, the Lord Jesus Christ"* (Phil. 3:20; NIV).

Both Ryrie and Walvoord were right when they say that some of the "everlasting" promises and covenants spoken of in the OT only apply to time and history and when time and history have come to an end and give way to a timeless eternity then those 'everlasting' promises and covenants will cease. That means that Israel's "everlasting" New Covenant will end and therefore it is not the same "eternal" *diathēkē* of Hebrews 13:20.

The Eternal *Diathēkē*

Let us now look at a passage which speaks of the eternal *Diathēkē* that is in operation today in the Body of Christ:

*"Now the God of peace, that brought again from the dead our Lord Jesus, that great shepherd of the sheep, through the blood of **the eternal testament**"* (Heb. 13:20-21; Jubilee Bible 2000).

The word "eternal" is translated from the Greek

word *aionios*, and that word means *"without end, never to cease, everlasting."* [14]

With that in mind it is not surprising to see the "gospel" described as being eternal:

*"Then I saw another angel flying in midair, and he had **the eternal gospel** to proclaim to those who live on the earth--to every nation, tribe, language and people."* (Rev. 14:6).

It is clear that the New *Diathēkē* which applies to the nation of Israel will indeed come to an end and therefore that *Diathēkē* or Covenant has absolutely nothing to do with the eternal New *Diathēkē* which is in effect now, the gospel.

These facts demonstrate once again that the two plans of God are mutually exclusive. Since the Divine plan toward Israel is "temporal" in nature then it cannot be said to be "eternal."

The author encourages questions, comments and edifying discussion. Please contact him via email: jerryshugart2@yahoo.com

End Notes

1. Lewis Sperry Chafer, *Systematic Theology*, 4:41.

2. Charles C. Ryrie, *Dispensationalism*, 134.

3. Andrew M. Woods, *The Coming Kingdom*, 262-63.

4. Roger M. Raymer, "1 Peter," in *The Bible*

Knowledge Commentary; New Testament, 842.

5. Sir Robert Anderson, *Types in Hebrews*, 52.

6. Ada R. Habershon, *Study of the Types* (Grand Rapids: Kregel Publications, 1993), 11.

7. Charles Fritsch, "Principles of Biblical Typology," in *Bibliotheca Sacra* 104, 1947, 220.

8. Henry W. Soltau, *The Tabernacle, the Priesthood and the Offerings* (Grand Rapids: Kregel Classics, 1994), 451.

9. Craig A. Blaising, *Progressive Dispensationalism*, 26.

10. *Ibid.*, 28-9.

11. *Ibid.*, 29-30.

12. Craig A. Blaising, *Progressive Dispensationalism*, 32.

13. *Ibid.*, 43-44.

14. Joseph Henry Thayer, *A Greek-English Lexicon of the New Testament*, 20.

www.ingramcontent.com/pod-product-compliance
Lightning Source LLC
Chambersburg PA
CBHW030712110426
R18122000003B/R181220PG42736CBX00010B/7